经典无删节版

图文美绘 双语典藏

假如给我三天光明

【美】海伦·凯勒 / 著　查文宏　项 艳 / 译

全国百佳出版社

图书在版编目（CIP）数据

假如给我三天光明 /（美）海伦·凯勒著；查文宏，项艳译. -- 南昌：江西人民出版社，2017.2
ISBN 978-7-210-08915-5

Ⅰ.①假… Ⅱ.①海…②查… Ⅲ.①凯勒 (Keller, Hellen 1880-1968) — 自传 Ⅳ.① K837.127=533

中国版本图书馆 CIP 数据核字（2016）第 269606 号

假如给我三天光明（图文美绘　双语典藏）
Three Days to See

（美）海伦·凯勒著；查文宏　项艳译

责任编辑：李月华
书籍设计：游　珑
出　　版．江西人民出版社
发　　行．各地新华书店
地　　址．江西省南昌市三经路 47 号附 1 号
编辑部电话：0791-86898143
发行部电话：0791-86898815
邮　　编：330006
网　　址：www.jxpph.com
E-mail：jxpph@tom.com　web@jxpph.com
2017 年 2 月第 1 版　　2017 年 2 月第 1 次印刷
开　本：1/16　720mm×1000mm
印　张：12
字　数：200 千字
ISBN 978-7-210-08915-5
定　价：35.00 元
承印厂：深圳精彩印联合印刷公司
赣版权登字—01—2016—836
版权所有　侵权必究
赣人版图书凡属印刷、装订错误，请随时向承印厂调换

前言

一场发现之旅
A journey of discovery

本书的第一部分是《假如给我三天光明》，它是海伦·凯勒的散文代表作。终其一生，凯勒只能用指尖感受自然与人世的千姿百态。她是如此渴望光明，如此期盼能目睹这个奇妙的世界。她的老师安妮·沙利文，是她要铭记一生的人，是她为她打开了世界的门窗，让她具备了解世界的能力。安妮·沙利文的成功是流芳百世的传奇。在她教授海伦学会写作之后不久，凯勒差不多就成了全美国的知名人士。

假如能有三天光明，第一天，凯勒当然首先要仔细端详睿智善良的沙利文老师，然后凝视亲朋好友的脸庞，看看狗狗和心爱的书籍，并到树林里漫步。第二天，要欣赏壮丽的日出，去博物馆感悟人类与自然的历史演变，徜徉在优雅的艺术品中，再去剧院观赏精彩的演出。她想感受世界的历史变迁和人类艺术的瑰丽奇壮。第三天，要在帝国大厦上俯瞰纽约市，逛逛繁华的商业街，还要去贫民窟、工厂和公园体察民情，将幸福和悲伤都收入眼底。

第二部分是海伦·凯勒的成长日记。在这里，我们可以阅读到海伦·凯勒的每一步成长，她接受了生命的挑战，以惊人的毅力面对环境，终于在黑暗中找到了光明，发现了真正的自我。不仅如此，她还以博爱的心灵关怀社会，以己之力向世界发声，尽力帮助那些和她一样身体残疾的人。通过阅读我们会发现，海伦·凯勒的故事不仅仅是一个简单的战胜厄运的故事，她从容面对生活的无常与挫折，一次次成功挑战生命的极限，成为第一个真正向全世界发出响亮声音的盲聋哑人，这是一个伟大而不平凡的故事。

目录

假如给我三天光明

一 指尖上的温柔演出　3

二 难忘人间温馨时光　6

三 徜徉于大都会艺术博物馆　9

四 帝国大厦之巅的惊鸿一瞥　14

我的成长日记

一 快乐的铅笔　35

二 美妙的世界　37

三 学习的乐趣　47

四 用嘴说话的快乐　71

五 为了小汤米　86

六 发表的文章　100

七 开始读唇训练　121

八 圆大学之梦　132

九 多彩的生活还在继续　175

假如给我三天光明

  光明，对普通人来说是习以为常的。清早醒来，展现在我们眼前的即是一个明亮世界。但你是否知道生活在寂静和黑暗中的盲聋人是多么渴望光明和声音啊？海伦·凯勒就是他们中的杰出一员。她用坚强乐观、积极进取的态度笑对人生。海伦大胆假设，假如有三天光明，她将好好珍惜这宝贵时光。作者的想象力十分丰富，虚构了她所不能看到的、听到的许多事物和场景，但正是这非现实的记叙、丰富的想象，让我们看到了作者一生急欲打开视听窗口的诚挚愿望。文章中，海伦用优美而传神的文字，善意批评了那些对美好事物麻木不仁的"有视力的人"，提醒人们要充分利用眼睛和其他感官，感受世间万物，关爱他人，快乐生活！

指尖上的温柔演出

我们大家都曾读过一些扣人心弦的故事，故事里的主人公只能活有限的、特定的一段时间。有时这段时间长达一年，有时则短为 24 小时。我们总是饶有兴趣地想看看，那些在劫难逃的人是如何度过他的最后一天或最后一小时的。当然，我所指的是有选择权的自由人，而不是那些已被定罪、活动范围受到严格限制的罪犯。

这类故事常令我们思索，如果处在相似的情况下，我们会怎么做？如果我们是即将赴死的人，在生命的最后时刻，我们脑海中会涌现出哪些事情、哪些经历和哪些想法呢？回顾往昔，我们能重寻哪些快乐，又有什么遗憾呢？

有时我会想，如果我们在过每一天时，都仿佛明天我们就将逝去似的，那么我们就更有可能遵循一条通往美好生活的准则。这种生活态度必将使我们更加珍惜生命的价值。我们会优雅而朝气蓬勃地过好每一天，并珍视那些在时光流逝中，离我们渐行渐远的美好回忆。当然，世间也有人是按享乐主义[1]的信条"吃、喝、玩、乐"来生活的，但当死神迫在眉睫时，大多数人都会有所改变的。

---

[1] epicurean motto 此处译为"享乐主义"。伊壁鸠鲁（Epicurus）是古希腊哲学家和无神论者，他认为生活的主要目的是享乐。

故事中，那些注定要死的主人公往往会在最后一刻受到命运的垂青而得救，但此后他的价值观常常也会发生改变，他对生活的意义及其永恒的精神价值会有更深的感悟。我们注意到，那些正生活在死亡阴影中，或曾跟死神擦肩而过的人们在做任何事情时，内心总是充满了喜悦。

可是，我们大多数人对生命的美好却不以为然。虽然我们知道，死亡注定会在某一天来临，但我们通常都把那天想象成遥远的未来。当我们健康快乐时，死亡似乎是遥不可及的，我们很少会去想它，只是日复一日地打发那无穷的时光。我们关注那些无聊的琐事，几乎很难意识到自己得过且过的生活态度。

我猜想，这种懒洋洋的生活态度会影响我们的感官和知觉。只有聋者才珍惜听力，只有盲人才能意识到视觉所带来的多姿多彩的快乐。那些在成年时失去视觉和听觉的人们尤其如此，而那些从没有遭受过视力或听力损伤的人却很少充分利用他们的天赋感官。他们的眼睛对周围的景观视而不见，耳朵对声音充耳不闻，往往心不在焉，毫无鉴赏力。老话说得好，只有失去时，才会懂得应该珍惜；只有生病时，才会懂得健康的可贵。

我常常想，如果每个人在他刚成年时，能有几天因病因伤而致盲和致聋，那将是一件因祸得福的事，黑暗会使他更加珍惜视力，寂静将教会他声音的美妙。

有时，我会试一试我那些视力良好的朋友，想知道他们看到了什么。最近，我的一位好朋友来看我，她刚经历了一次丛林漫步之旅，我问她观察到了什么，她答道："没什么特别的。"如果不是因为我对这种回答已习以为常的话，我一定会对她的话深表怀疑。其实很久以前，我就知道看得见的人往往是熟视无睹的。

这怎么可能呢？我自问：在树林里走了一小时，却没看见任何值得注意的东西？而我，一位看不见的人，仅仅通过触摸，却能发现成千上万件有趣的东西。我能感觉出一片树叶精妙的对称。我曾用手爱抚过一株白桦树光洁的树干，也触摸过松树那凹凸不平的粗糙树皮。春天，我满怀希望地抚摸枝条寻找嫩芽，那是大自然在冬天的酣睡之后醒来的第一个标志。我感受过花朵天鹅绒般宜人的柔软质地，和它们那奇妙的造型；还感受过大自然展露给我的奇观。偶尔，机缘巧合，当我把手轻轻放在一棵小树上时，还能感受到一只聚精会神歌唱的小鸟的欢快震颤。我会欣然让清凉的小溪水在我张开的指缝间奔流。我喜欢松针铺成的绿绒地毯和海绵般富有弹性的草地，却不喜欢奢华的波斯地毯。在我看来，季节变换的盛况就是一部激动人心、永不落幕的戏剧，我能用自己的指尖来感受它的一幕幕演出。

有时，我的心会因为渴望看到这一切而哭泣。如果我仅凭触觉就能感受到这么多快乐，那么如果通过视觉，岂不是能发现更多美好的事物？可是，那些有视觉的人往往所见甚少，他们对世间五彩缤纷的色彩和景象熟视无睹。也许只有人类才会对我们已拥有的一切不加珍惜，对我们没有的却孜孜以求。然而，在这明亮的世界里，如果仅仅把天赋的视力当作一种便利，而不是用来为生活增添情趣，那么这将是一个大大的遗憾。

如果我是一所大学的校长，我就要开设一门名为"如何应用你的眼睛"的必修课。这门课的教授将向学生们展示，通过实实在在地观察那些他们以前无动于衷的事物，他们的生活将会增添多少欢乐。教授将努力唤醒学生们那处于休眠状态的、充满惰性的感官。

难忘人间温馨时光

如果我能有机会使用我的眼睛,哪怕仅仅只用三天,那么我也要对自己最希望看见的东西做详尽的阐述。当然,在我处于想象之中时,请你也全神贯注地来思考这个问题:如果你仅有三天时间可以看东西,那么你该如何使用你的眼睛呢?如果在第三天晚上,黑暗就将扑面而来,而你也知道,太阳将永不在你眼前升起,那么你该如何度过这宝贵的三天呢?你最想让目光流连何处呢?

对我而言,自然最想看到是那些在经年累月的黑暗中令我日渐珍惜的事物。你肯定也想把你的目光久久停留在那些你所珍惜的事物上。这样,你就能在暗夜隐隐出现之前,将它们铭刻在自己的记忆之中。

如果因某种奇迹,我被馈赠了能看见光明的三天时间,之后又将陷入万劫不复的黑暗之中,那么我会把这段时间分为三部分。

第一天,我要看看那些用善良、温柔和陪伴为我生命赋予价值的人们。首先,我将长久地凝视我亲爱的老师,安妮·沙利文·梅西夫人的脸庞。当我还是个孩子时,她就来到了我身边,为我开启了外面的世界。我不仅要观察她脸庞的轮廓,将其珍藏在记忆深处,而且还要研究她的脸庞,找到她在承担教育我这一艰巨任务时,从她脸上所流露出的同情、温柔和耐心等生动表情。我想从她的眼睛里看到性格的力量,正是这一力量使她在困难面前坚韧不拔;我还想看看她时常展露给我的、对全人类的悲悯情怀。

我不知道怎样才能通过"心灵之窗"——眼睛,来透视朋友的内心。我只能用自己的指尖来"看"一张脸的轮廓,但我可以探测到欢笑、悲伤和其他许多明显的感情。通过抚摸朋友的脸,我能认识他们,可我不能依靠触摸来勾勒出他们的真正个性。当然，通过某些方法，比如他们表达给我的思想、他们表露给我的各种行为，我可以了解他们的个性，但我终究无法对他们做进一步的了解。我相信，只有亲眼看到他们，通过观察他们对各种思想和环境的反应，捕捉他们眼中和脸上那转瞬即逝的神色，才可能使我对他们有更深的了解。

我很了解我身边的朋友，因为随着岁月流逝，他们已全方位地向我展示了自身的变化；但对于偶遇的朋友，我只能通过与其握手，用指尖触摸他们的嘴唇感知他们的话语，以及他们在我掌心轻敲的句子来获得一个不完整的印象。

对于有视觉的你们来说，可以通过观察他人表情的微妙变化、肌肉的颤抖和手的摆动来迅速地领悟他的意图，这是非常容易，也非常能令你们满足的事。但是，你们可曾想过用目光去透视一位朋友或熟人的内心？难道你们中的大多数人不都是漫不经心地瞟一眼别人，仅在对其外部特征有大致了解后，就转移目光了吗？

例如，你们能准确地描述出五位好友的面容吗？我想你们中有些人可以，但大多数人做不到。我曾做过实验，询问几位与妻子长期生活在一起的丈夫们知不知道他们妻子眼睛的颜色，结果这些丈夫往往显得尴尬而困惑，并承认他们不知道。顺便说一下，有些妻子往往会不停地抱怨其丈夫从不注意她们的新衣服、新帽子以及家中摆设的变化。

看得见的人，其眼睛对周围的事物很快就会习以为常。他们实际上仅会注意那些令人惊奇的事情和壮观的景物。但是，即使他们在观看壮观的景物时，他们的目光也是懒散的。从每天的法庭记录中，我们都能看出"目击证人"看得非常不准。一个案件会被几个证人以几种不同的方式"看见"。有些人看的是比别人多些，但几乎没人能完全看见其视线范围内发生的一切。

哦，假如仅给我三天光明，我将能看见多少东西啊！

第一天将会是忙碌的一天。我要把所有亲爱的朋友都请来，久久凝视他们的脸庞，把展示他们内在美的外部特征牢牢镌

刻在脑海里。我也会把目光停留在一名婴儿的脸上,捕捉他那热情洋溢、天真无邪的美。这时的婴儿,还不具有在日后生活的磨砺中才会树立起来的个人意识。

我还想看看我的狗狗们那忠诚、可信赖的眼睛——那严肃而狡猾的小长毛猎狗达吉,还有强健而善解人意的丹麦种大狗海尔格,它们曾给予我的热情、温柔、嬉戏和友谊,对我是莫大的安慰。

在这忙碌的第一天,我还要看看家中朴素的小物品,我要看看脚下小地毯的温馨色彩、墙上的画和那些将房子变成家的私密小饰品。我的目光将会怀着敬意落在我读过的凸字盲文书上,但我更急切、更感兴趣地是要看看那些有视觉的人所读的印刷书籍。在我生命的漫漫长夜里,那些我曾读过的书和别人读给我的书,已塑造出一座璀璨雄伟的灯塔,熠熠生辉,照亮了我人生及心灵最深远的航道。

在第一天下午,我将久久地在树林里漫步,自然界的美景将使我的双眼陶醉。在几小时里,我会贪婪地饱览那些曾展现在有视觉的人面前的辉煌壮丽的景色。在结束这次游览的归途中,我要走靠近农场的小径,这样,我就有可能看到耐心的马儿在田野里耕作(或许我只能看到一台拖拉机吧!),并看到与土壤紧密相依的人们宁静而安详的生活方式。我还会为五彩斑斓的落日奇观而祈祷。

夜幕降临,我将体验在人造灯光下看景物的双重喜悦。当大自然被黑暗执掌时,人类中的天才们却创造出了灯光,从而拓展了人们的视力范围。

在能看见的第一天晚上,我将无法入眠,脑海中会一直浮现对这一天的美好记忆。

三 徜徉于大都会艺术博物馆

第二天——能看见的第二天——我要黎明即起,去观看那惊心动魄的黑夜变为白昼的奇迹。当太阳唤醒沉睡的大地时,我将怀着敬畏之心,观赏霞光万丈的辉煌景色。

这一天,我将专注地向世界、过去和现在投上匆匆一瞥。我要看看那展现人类进步的恢宏展览和万花筒般千变万化的时代变迁。但如此浩如烟海的长卷,如何能压缩在一天内看完?当然,只有去博物馆了。我曾多次参观过纽约的自然历史博物馆[①],用手触摸过不少展品。但我一直渴望能在那里亲眼看看浓缩的地球史和陈列的地球居民——即原生环境下的各种动物和各类人种的画像。我想目睹恐龙和乳齿象的硕大骨架,早在人类出现以前,它们就在地球上漫游,但人类却凭借其小巧的身材和睿智的大脑,征服了动物王国。我还想看看动物和人类进化过程的真实再现,人类为使自己在地球上的家园更安全而不断制作改进的种种工具,以及自然历史的方方面面。

我想知道,本文的读者中,有多少人曾在这座启迪心智的博物馆里观赏过画像上的泱泱万物。当然,很多人都没有这种机会,但我确信许多有机会的人却没有好好利用它。在这里,你的确应该仔细地用眼睛去看。目光敏锐

---

① 指美国自然历史博物馆,位于纽约曼哈顿,始建于1869年,是世界上规模最大的自然史博物馆。

的你可以在这里度过许多收获颇丰的日子。可我,仅有假想的三天能看见,所以我在这只能匆匆一瞥,然后赶往别处。

我的下一站是大都会艺术博物馆②,正如自然历史博物馆展示了世界的物质领域,大都会艺术博物馆则全方位地展现了人类的精神领域。纵观人类历史,对艺术表达的渴求几乎与对食物、居所和繁殖的渴求是一样的,都对人类社会的发展产生了强大的推动力。就在这里,在大都会艺术博物馆宏大的展室里,埃及、希腊和罗马的精神通过艺术作品,呈现在我面前。我凭借双手,完美感知了古代尼罗河沃土上的男神和女神们的雕像;我抚摸了巴台农神庙③带状装饰的复制品;我感受到了雅典勇士冲锋时的优美节奏;我用指尖与阿波罗、维纳斯和萨莫色雷斯胜利女神像④亲密接触。我对荷马那满是皱纹、留着胡须的面孔倍感亲切,因为他也深知失明的滋味。

我的双手恋恋不舍地停留在罗马帝国及其后期的那些栩栩如生的大理石雕塑上;我用双手抚过米开朗琪罗⑤塑造的、那鼓舞人心的英雄摩西的石膏模型;我感知了罗丹⑥的力量;我对哥特式木制雕刻品所蕴含的一丝不苟的精神肃然起敬。这些能够触摸的艺术品对我而言意义非凡。但它们是用来观

---

②大都会艺术博物馆位于美国纽约,与著名的美国自然历史博物馆遥遥相对。收藏有超过三百万件的非洲、亚洲、大洋洲、拜占庭和伊斯兰艺术品。

③巴台农神庙是希腊用以祭祀雅典娜女神的神庙,相传建于公元前447年。

④萨莫色雷斯岛位于爱琴海东北部,其上有1863年发现的著名的胜利女神雕像,是公元前2世纪最佳雕塑之一。

⑤米开朗琪罗·博那罗蒂(1475—1564),意大利文艺复兴时期伟大的绘画家、雕塑家、建筑师和诗人,文艺复兴时期雕塑艺术最高峰的代表。与拉斐尔和达·芬奇并称为"文艺复兴后三杰"。

⑥奥古斯特·罗丹(1840—1917),法国雕塑艺术家。被认为是19世纪和20世纪初最伟大的现实主义雕塑艺术家。

赏的，而不是用来触摸的。对那些潜藏在我眼前的美，我只能去猜测。我能欣赏希腊花瓶的简洁线条，却无从感知它精美的装饰图案。

所以，在我能看见的第二天，我将试图通过艺术家们的作品来探索其灵魂。现在，我能看见那些我仅能凭借触摸去了解的物品了。更令我欣喜的是，整个辉煌的油画世界都将向我敞开大门：从有虔诚宗教信仰的文艺复兴前的画家的作品，到有着强烈视觉冲击力的现代艺术。我将细细鉴赏拉斐尔⑦、达·芬奇⑧、提香⑨、伦布兰⑩的油画；我要让双眼享受意大利维罗纳人的温馨色彩盛宴；我要研究幻想风格主义画家艾尔·格列柯⑪的神秘；并从法国风景画大师柯罗⑫那里捕捉大自然的清新美景。啊，对你们有视觉的人来说，在这里可以观赏到多少富有内涵的精美艺术品啊！

匆匆游览完上述艺术神殿，我对它只得到一个肤浅的印象，仍不能对展现在你们面前的那个博大艺术世界做任何评论。艺术家告诉我，为了拥有深邃而精准的艺术鉴赏力，人们必须训练眼力。人们必须通过学习，才会懂得如何凭经验来衡量线条、构图、外形和颜色的水准。如果我有视力，就能从事如此令人着迷的研究，那该是多么幸福啊！但我却听说，对于许多有视觉

---

⑦拉斐尔·桑西（1483—1520），意大利著名画家，"文艺复兴后三杰"中最年轻的一位。

⑧达·芬奇（1452—1519），欧洲文艺复兴时期的天才科学家、发明家、画家。现代学者称他为"文艺复兴时期最完美的代表"。

⑨提香·韦切利奥（1490—1576），被誉为"西方油画之父"，是意大利文艺复兴后期威尼斯画派的代表画家。

⑩伦布兰（1609—1669），荷兰画家。

⑪艾尔·格列柯（1541—1614），西班牙文艺复兴时期著名的幻想风格主义画家。

⑫柯罗（1796—1875），是法国的前印象派画家，被认为是法国的风景画大师。

的人而言，艺术世界仍是他们未曾探索过，也未曾从中获过教益的一片茫茫黑夜。

要让我离开大都会艺术博物馆，离开这配有美之钥匙、充盈着被忽略的美的博物馆，我是极不情愿的。但是，有视觉的人并不是一定要到大都会艺术博物馆才能找到这枚美之钥匙。在小型博物馆和小图书馆的书籍里，同样躺着相似的钥匙，等待着你们去发现。但在我假想的、能看见的有限时间里，我自然要选择一块宝地，用这把钥匙，在最短的时间内去开启最大的宝库。

我要在剧院或电影院度过我能看见的第二个夜晚。时至今日，虽然我经常参加各种戏剧演出，但事先都要由同伴将剧情拼写在我手上，我才能理解。我多么渴望能亲眼看看那魅力四射的哈姆雷特和穿着伊丽莎白女王时代的彩色礼服、充满活力的福斯泰夫啊！我多么想目不转睛地盯着哈姆雷特的每一个优雅举止、盯着精神饱满的福斯泰夫的每一次昂首阔步啊！虽然我想看几十部戏，但却只能选一部，这真让我难以抉择啊！你们有视觉的人可以随意看自己喜欢的戏，但我想知道，当你们观赏一部戏剧、电影或其他表演时，你们中有几个人能意识到正是视觉的奇迹才使你们能享受色彩、仪态和动作之美？又有几人会对此心存感激呢？

由于我的感官被限制在一个仅能用双手触摸的范围内，所以我不能享受到抑扬顿挫的节奏之美。我只能朦朦胧胧地想象芭蕾舞舞蹈家巴甫洛娃[13]的优雅，当然我对欢快的节奏也略知一二，因为我常常能通过震动地板的音乐来感受到它的节拍。我猜想那些有节奏的动作，一定很令人兴奋。通过用手

[13] 安娜·巴甫洛娃（1881—1931），出生于圣彼得堡一个贫民家庭，是20世纪初芭蕾舞坛的一颗巨星，为在全球传播、普及芭蕾艺术做出了不可估量的贡献。

指追踪大理石雕像的线条，我能积累一些认识。如果这种静态的优雅都如此可爱，那么能目睹动态的优雅一定会更让人震撼。

我最珍视的一幕记忆是：当约瑟夫·杰弗逊在扮演他心爱的角色瑞普·凡·温克尔时，同意我在他表演一些姿势和说话时，去摸他的脸庞和双手。这使我多少能领略到一点戏剧世界的浮光掠影，我将永不会忘记那快乐的瞬间。但是，哦，我错过了多少东西啊！你们有视觉的人通过观看戏剧表演的动作和倾听人物对白，能从中获得多少欢愉啊！如果我能亲眼看一部戏，我就会知道怎样在心中描绘出我曾读过的剧本，或畅想出那些我依靠手语字母了解到的戏剧场景。

因此，在我假想的能看见的第二个夜晚，那些戏剧文学中的伟大人物将把睡眠从我眼中挤走，我要抓紧时间欣赏戏剧。

四

帝国大厦之巅的惊鸿一瞥

接下来的清晨,我又将迎着黎明,急切地去找寻新的欢愉。我坚信,对于那些用心去看的有视觉的人,每天的黎明都会展现出永恒的新美景。

按照我想象的奇迹中的假设条件,这将是我能看见的第三天,也是最后一天。我不能把时间浪费在遗憾和渴望中,我还有太多的东西要看。我把第一天奉献给了我的那些生机勃勃或无生命的朋友们。第二天,人类与自然的历史展示在我面前。今天,我将在现实世界度过一个普通的工作日,在熙熙攘攘的人群中体验职业生活。在像纽约这样的地方,如何能找到活动最多、最容易体察人们生活状况的区域呢?只有城市才是我的目的地。

我的家位于长岛森林小丘住宅区,这里是宁静可爱的郊区,芳草茵茵,鲜花盛开,绿树环绕。一座座小巧整洁的房子,飘荡着妇女和儿童们的欢声笑语,它们是那些在城里辛勤劳作的人们静谧的憩息港湾。我从家中出发,驱车驶过横跨在东河上的钢结构悬索桥,对人类的聪明才智和创造力又有了新的、惊人的发现和体验。忙碌的船只在河面上"嘎嘎"地往来穿梭——既有高速飞驶的快艇,又有笨头笨脑、"突突"喷气的拖轮。如果今后我还能看得见,那么我一定要用更多时间来欣赏这条河的宜人景色。

我仰望前方,眼前鳞次栉比地耸立着奇异的摩天大楼,纽约仿佛是座从童话故事书页中崛起的城市。这是多么令人惊叹的奇观啊!那些熠熠闪光的尖塔,那些钢筋和石头砌成的宏伟银行——它们结构精巧,看上去就像是神仙们为自己建造的!这生机勃勃的美景展现的正是千千万万人日常生活的一部分。我想知道有多少人会对它投上匆匆一瞥。恐怕寥寥无几吧。因为他们对这壮丽的景色非常熟悉,早已经视而不见了。

我急切地爬上巨型建筑——帝国大厦①的顶端。前不久，我曾在这里通过我秘书的眼睛"俯瞰"这座城市，我热切地想比较一下自己的想象和现实的差异。我相信，展现在眼前的景色一定不会令我失望，因为对我而言，这完全是另一个世界的奇观。

接着，我开始环游这座城市。首先，我站在繁华的街角，仅仅是看看行人，试图通过目测来了解一些他们的生活。每当看到微笑的人，我就感到快乐；看到认真抉择的人，我会感到骄傲；而看到痛苦的人，我也深表同情。

我沿着第五大道②漫步，目光游移，并未专注于某一特殊目标，于是我看到了万花筒般五彩缤纷的颜色。我相信，在人群中行走的妇女们，她们的服装颜色一定是一幅让我永不厌倦的绚丽画卷。如果我能看见的话，我很可能会像其他妇女一样，对某件服装的式样和裁剪非常感兴趣，却不太注意整体的华丽色彩。并且我还相信，我将成为一位有瘾的橱窗浏览者③，因为，能用眼睛去欣赏琳琅满目的展示商品，是多么令人快乐的事啊！

从第五大道起，我游览了全城——去了公园大道、贫民窟、工厂和孩子们嬉戏的公园。通过参观外国居民区，我进行了一次不出国的海外旅行。我始终睁大眼睛，将幸福和悲伤都收入眼底，这样我才能深入调查，进一步了解人们是如何工作和生活的。我的心中充满了形形色色的人和事。我的眼睛密切地关注每件事，决不轻易放过一件小事。有些景象赏心悦目，使人快乐；但有些则凄惨糟糕，令人伤心。即使面对后者，我也绝不闭上我的双眼，因为它们也是生活的一部分。如果对它们视而不见，就等于失

---

①帝国大厦为纽约市著名的地标和旅游景点之一，被美国土木工程师学会评价为现代世界七大工程奇迹之一。

②第五大道是美国纽约市曼哈顿一条重要的南北向干道，景点众多，有帝国大厦、纽约公共图书馆、洛克菲勒中心、圣帕特里克教堂以及中央公园等。这里聚集了许多著名的品牌商店，又被称为"梦之街"，是高级购物街区。

③橱窗浏览者指只逛不买的人。

去了仁爱友善之心。

我能看见光明的第三天即将结束了。也许我该把剩余的几小时奉献给许多重要事务。但是，在最后一个夜晚，恐怕我还是会再次跑向剧院，去欣赏一场滑稽有趣的戏剧，从而感悟喜剧是如何诠释人性的光辉的。

午夜时分，对我失明的短暂缓刑就要结束，永恒的黑夜即将降临。当然，在这短短的三天里，我无法看完自己想看的一切。只有当黑暗再次向我袭来之时，我才意识到我还有多少东西没来得及看，但我的心中已盈满美好的回忆，所以我不会浪费时间去后悔。今后，每当我触摸一件物品时，鲜活的记忆都将重现这物品的外观。

如果你知道自己即将突然失明，那么你做的计划也许跟我对重见光明的这三天所做的计划是不同的。但我相信，假如你真的面临那种厄运，那么在长夜降临之前，你的双眼将专注于以前从未见过的事物，并将它们储存在记忆中。你会竭尽全力地用好双眼。你所看到的一切，对你而言都是极其宝贵的，你的目光将投向出现在你视力范围内的每一件物品。最终，你将会真正看见，眼前展现的是一个崭新的美好世界。

失明的我想给那些看得见的人们——那些能够充分利用其视觉禀赋的人们一个忠告：善用你的眼睛吧！仿佛明天你将突然失明似的。同时，也要好好使用其他感官。认真聆听音乐之声、鸟儿鸣唱和雄浑的管弦乐吧！仿佛明天你将突然耳聋似的。仔细抚摸每一件你想要抚摸的物品吧！仿佛明天你的触觉将不复存在似的。闻闻芬芳的花朵，尝尝美味的佳肴吧，仿佛明天你将失去嗅觉和味觉似的。好好使用每一个感官，通过大自然赋予你的几种感觉方式，去淋漓尽致地感知世界展示给你的所有愉悦和美好吧！不过，在所有感觉中，我相信，视觉一定会带给你最多的欢乐。

Three Days to See

All of us have read thrilling stories in which the hero had only a limited and specified time to live. Sometimes it was as long as a year; sometimes as short as twenty-four hours. But always we were interested in discovering just how the doomed man chose to spend his last days or his last hours. I speak, of course, of free men who have a choice, not condemned criminals whose sphere of activities is strictly delimited.

Such stories set us thinking, wondering what we should do under similar circumstances. What events, what experiences, what associations, should we crowd into those last hours as mortal beings? What happiness should we find in reviewing the past, what regrets?

Sometimes I have thought it would be an excellent rule to live each day as if we should die tomorrow. Such an attitude would emphasize sharply the values of life. We should live each day with a gentleness, a vigor, and a keenness of appreciation which are often lost when time stretches before us in the constant panorama of more days and months and years to come. There are those, of course, who would adopt the epicurean motto of 'Eat, drink, and be merry,' but most people would be chastened by the certainty of impending death.

In stories, the doomed hero is usually saved at the last minute by some stroke

of fortune, but almost always his sense of values is changed. He becomes more appreciative of the meaning of life and its permanent spiritual values. It has often been noted that those who live, or have lived, in the shadow of death bring a mellow sweetness to everything they do.

Most of us, however, take life for granted. We know that one day we must die, but usually we picture that day as far in the future. When we are in buoyant health, death is all but unimaginable. We seldom think of it. The days stretch out in an endless vista. So we go about our petty tasks, hardly aware of our listless attitude toward life.

The same lethargy, I am afraid, characterizes the use of all our faculties and senses. Only the deaf appreciate hearing, only the blind realize the manifold blessings that lie in sight. Particularly does this observation apply to those who have lost sight and hearing in adult life. But those who have never suffered impairment of sight or hearing seldom make the fullest use of these blessed faculties. Their eyes and ears take in all sights and sounds hazily, without concentration and with little appreciation. It is the same old story of not being grateful for what we have until we lose it, of not being conscious of health until we are ill.

I have often thought it would be a blessing if each human being were stricken blind and deaf for a few days at some time during his early adult life. Darkness would make him more appreciative of sight; silence would teach him the joys of sound.

Now and then I have tested my seeing friends to discover what they see. Recently I was visited by a very good friend who had just returned from a long walk in the woods, and I asked her what she had observed. "Nothing in particular," she replied. I might have been incredulous had I not been accustomed to such responses, for long ago I became convinced that the seeing see little.

How was it possible, I asked myself, to walk for an hour through the woods and see nothing worthy of note? I who cannot see find hundreds of things to interest me through mere touch. I feel the delicate symmetry of a leaf. I pass my hands lovingly about the smooth skin of a silver birch, or the rough, shaggy bark of a pine. In spring I touch the branches of trees hopefully in search of a bud, the first sign of awakening Nature after her winter's sleep. I feel the delightful, velvety texture of a flower, and discover its remarkable convolutions; and something of the miracle of Nature is revealed to me. Occasionally, if I am very fortunate, I place my hand gently on a small tree and feel the happy quiver of a bird in full song. I am delighted to have the cool waters of a brook rush through my open fingers. To me a lush carpet of pine needles or spongy grass is more welcome than the most luxurious Persian rug. To me the pageant of seasons is a thrilling and unending drama, the action of which streams through my finger tips.

At times my heart cries out with longing to see all these things. If I can get so much pleasure from mere touch, how much more beauty must be revealed by sight. Yet, those who have eyes apparently see little. The panorama of color and action which fills the world is taken for granted. It is human, perhaps, to appreciate little that which we have and to long for that which we have not, but it is a great pity that in the world of light the gift of sight is used only as a mere convenience rather than as a means of adding fullness to life.

If I were the president of a university I should establish a compulsory course in "How to Use Your Eyes." The professor would try to show his pupils how they could add joy to their lives by really seeing what passes unnoticed before them. He would try to awake their dormant and sluggish faculties.

Perhaps I can best illustrate by imagining what I should most like to see if I were given the use of my eyes, say, for just three days. And while I am imagining, suppose you, too, set your mind to work on the problem of how you would use your own eyes if you had only three more days to see. If with the oncoming darkness of the third night you knew that the sun would never rise for you again, how would you spend those three precious intervening days? What would you most want to let your gaze rest upon?

I, naturally, should want most to see the things which have become dear to me through my years of darkness. You, too, would want to let your eyes rest long on the things that have become dear to you so that you could take the memory of them with you into the night that loomed before you.

If, by some miracle, I were granted three seeing days, to be followed by a relapse into darkness, I should divide the period into three parts.

On the first day, I should want to see the people whose kindness and gentleness and companionship have made my life worth living. First I should like to gaze long upon the face of my dear teacher, Mrs. Anne Sullivan Macy, who came to me when I was a child and opened the outer world to me. I should want not merely to see the outline of her face, so that I could cherish it in my memory, but to study that face and find in it the living evidence of the sympathetic tenderness and patience with which she accomplished the difficult task of my education. I should like to see in her eyes that strength of character which has enabled her to stand firm in the face of difficulties, and that compassion for all humanity which she has revealed to me so often.

I do not know what it is to see into the heart of a friend through that "window of the soul," the eye. I can only "see" through my finger tips the outline of a face. I can detect laughter, sorrow, and many other obvious emotions. I know my friends from the feel of their faces. But I cannot really picture their personalities by touch. I know their personalities, of course, through other means, through the thoughts they express to me, through whatever of their actions are revealed to me. But I am denied that deeper understanding of them which I am sure would come through sight of them, through watching their reactions to various expressed thoughts and circumstances, through noting the immediate and fleeting reactions of their eyes and countenance.

Friends who are near to me I know well, because through the months and years they reveal themselves to me in all their phases; but of casual friends I have only an incomplete impression, an impression gained from a handclasp, from spoken words which I take from their lips with my finger tips, or which they tap into the palm of my hand.

How much easier, how much more satisfying it is for you who can see to grasp quickly the essential qualities of another person by watching the subtleties of expression, the quiver of a muscle, the flutter of a hand. But does it ever occur to you to use your sight to see into the inner nature of a friend or acquaintance? Do not most of you seeing people grasp casually the outward features of a face and let it go at that?

For instance, can you describe accurately the faces of five good friends? Some of you can, but many cannot. As an experiment, I have questioned husbands of long standing about the color of their wives' eyes, and often they express embarrassed confusion and admit that they do not know. And, incidentally, it is a chronic complaint of wives that their husbands do not notice new dresses, new hats, and changes in household arrangements.

The eyes of seeing persons soon become accustomed to the routine of their surroundings, and they actually see only the startling and spectacular. But even in viewing the most spectacular sights the eyes are lazy. Court records reveal every day how inaccurately "eyewitnesses" see. A given event will be "seen" in several different ways by as many witnesses. Some see more than others, but few see everything that is within the range of their vision.

Oh, the things that I should see if I had the power of sight for just three days!

The first day would be a busy one. I should call to me all my dear friends and look long into their faces, imprinting upon my mind the outward evidences of the beauty that is within them. I should let my eyes rest, too, on the face of a baby, so that I could catch a vision of the eager, innocent beauty which precedes the individual's consciousness of the conflicts which life develops.

And I should like to look into the loyal, trusting eyes of my dogs — the grave, canny little Scottie, Darkie, and the stalwart, understanding Great Dane, Helga, whose warm, tender, and playful friendships are so comforting to me.

On that busy first day I should also view the small simple things of my home. I want to see the warm colors in the rugs under my feet, the pictures on the walls, the intimate trifles that transform a house into home. My eyes would rest respectfully on the books in raised type which I have read, but they would be more eagerly interested in the printed books which seeing people can read, for during the long night of my life the books I have read and those which have been read to me have built themselves into a great shining lighthouse, revealing to me the deepest channels of human life and the human spirit.

In the afternoon of that first seeing day, I should take a long walk in the woods and intoxicate my eyes on the beauties of the world of Nature, trying desperately to absorb in a few hours the vast splendor which is constantly unfolding itself to those who can see. On the way home from my woodland jaunt my path would lie near a farm so that I might see the patient horses ploughing in the field (perhaps I should see only a tractor!) and the serene content of men living close to the soil. And I should pray for the glory of a colorful sunset.

When dusk had fallen, I should experience the double delight of being able to see by artificial light, which the genius of man has created to extend the power of his sight when Nature decrees darkness.

In the night of that first day of sight, I should not be able to sleep, so full would be my mind of the memories of the day.

III

The next day — the second day of sight — I should arise with the dawn and see the thrilling miracle by which night is transformed into day. I should behold with awe the magnificent panorama of light with which the sun awakens the sleeping earth.

This day I should devote to a hasty glimpse of the world, past and present. I should want to see the pageant of man's progress, the kaleidoscope of the ages. How can so much be compressed into one day? Through the museums, of course. Often I have visited the New York Museum of Natural History to touch with my hands many of the objects there exhibited, but I have longed to see with my eyes the condensed history of the earth and its inhabitants displayed there — animals and the races of men pictured in their native environment; gigantic carcasses of dinosaurs and mastodons which roamed the earth long before man appeared, with his tiny stature and powerful brain, to conquer the animal kingdom; realistic presentations of the processes of evolution in animals, in man, and in the implements which man has used to fashion for himself a secure home on this planet; and a thousand and one other aspects of natural history.

I wonder how many readers of this article have viewed this panorama of the face of living things as pictured in that inspiring museum. Many, of course, have not had the opportunity, but I am sure that many who have had the opportunity have not made use of it. There, indeed, is a place to use your eyes. You who see can spend many fruitful days there, but I, with my imaginary three days of sight, could only take a hasty glimpse, and pass on.

My next stop would be the Metropolitan Museum of Art, for just as the Museum of Natural History reveals the material aspects of the world, so does the Metropolitan show the myriad facets of the human spirit. Throughout the history of humanity the urge to artistic expression has been almost as powerful as the urge for food, shelter, and procreation. And here, in the vast chambers of the Metropolitan Museum, is unfolded before me the spirit of Egypt, Greece, and Rome, as expressed in their art. I know well through my hands the sculptured gods and goddesses of the ancient Nile land. I have felt copies of Parthenon friezes, and I have sensed the rhythmic beauty of charging Athenian warriors. Apollos and Venuses and the Winged Victory of Samothrace are friends of my finger tips. The gnarled, bearded features of Homer are dear to me, for he, too, knew blindness.

My hands have lingered upon the living marble of Roman sculpture as well as that of later generations. I have passed my hands over a plaster cast of Michelangelo's inspiring and heroic Moses; I have sensed the power of Rodin; I have been awed by the devoted spirit of Gothic wood carving. These arts which can be touched have meaning for me, but even they were meant to be seen rather than felt, and I can only guess at the beauty which remains hidden from me. I can admire the simple lines of a Greek vase, but its figured decorations are lost to me.

So on this, my second day of sight, I should try to probe into the soul of man through his art. The things I knew through touch I should now see. More splendid still, the whole magnificent world of painting would be opened to me, from the Italian Primitives, with their serene religious devotion, to the Moderns, with their feverish visions. I should look deep into the canvases of Raphael, Leonardo da Vinci, Titian, Rembrandt. I should want to feast my eyes upon the warm colors of Veronese, study the mysteries of El Greco, catch a new vision of Nature from Corot. Oh, there is so much rich meaning and beauty in the art of the ages for you who have eyes to see!

Upon my short visit to this temple of art I should not be able to review a fraction of that great world of art which is open to you. I should be able to get only a superficial impression. Artists tell me that for a deep and true appreciation of art one must educate the eye. One must learn through experience to weigh the merits of line, of composition, of form and color. If I had eyes, how happily would I embark upon so fascinating a study! Yet I am told that, to many of you who have eyes to see, the world of art is a dark night, unexplored and unilluminated.

It would be with extreme reluctance that I should leave the Metropolitan Museum, which contains the key to beauty — a beauty so neglected. Seeing persons, however, do not need a Metropolitan to find this key to beauty. The same key lies waiting in smaller museums, and in books on the shelves of even small libraries. But naturally, in my limited time of imaginary sight, I should choose the place where the key unlocks the greatest treasures in the shortest time.

The evening of my second day of sight I should spend at a theatre or at the movies. Even now I often attend theatrical performances of all sorts, but the action of the play must be spelled into my hand by a companion. But how I should like to see with my own eyes the fascinating figure of Hamlet, or the gusty Falstaff amid colorful Elizabethan trappings! How I should like to follow each movement of the graceful Hamlet, each strut of the hearty Falstaff! And since I could see only one play, I should be confronted by a many-horned dilemma, for there are scores of plays I should want to see. You who have eyes can see any you like. How many of you, I wonder, when you gaze at a play, a movie, or any spectacle, realize and give thanks for the miracle of sight which enables you to enjoy its color, grace, and movement?

I cannot enjoy the beauty of rhythmic movement except in a sphere restricted to the touch of my hands. I can vision only dimly the grace of a Pavlowa, although I know something of the delight of rhythm, for often I can sense the beat of music as it vibrates through the floor. I can well imagine that cadenced motion must be one of the most pleasing sights in the world. I have been able to gather something of this by tracing with my fingers the lines in sculptured marble; if this static grace can be so lovely, how much more acute must be the thrill of seeing grace in motion.

One of my dearest memories is of the time when Joseph Jefferson allowed me to touch his face and hands as he went through some of the gestures and speeches of his beloved Rip Van Winkle. I was able to catch thus a meagre glimpse of the world of drama, and I shall never forget the delight of that moment. But, oh, how much I must miss, and how much pleasure you seeing ones can derive from watching and hearing the interplay of speech and movement in the unfolding of a dramatic performance! If I could see only one play, I should know how to picture in my mind the action of a hundred plays which I have read or had transferred to me through the medium of the manual alphabet.

So, through the evening of my second imaginary day of sight, the great figures of dramatic literature would crowd sleep from my eyes.

IV

The following morning, I should again greet the dawn, anxious to discover new delights, for I am sure that, for those who have eyes which really see, the dawn of each day must be a perpetually new revelation of beauty.

This, according to the terms of my imagined miracle, is to be my third and last day of sight. I shall have no time to waste in regrets or longings; there is too much to see. The first day I devoted to my friends, animate and inanimate. The second revealed to me the history of man and Nature. Today I shall spend in the workaday world of the present, amid the haunts of men going about the business of life. And where can one find so many activities and conditions of men as in New York? So the city becomes my destination.

I start from my home in the quiet little suburb of Forest Hills, Long Island. Here, surrounded by green lawns, trees, and flowers, are neat little houses, happy with the voices and movements of wives and children, havens of peaceful rest for men who toil in the city. I drive across the lacy structure of steel which spans the East River, and I get a new and startling vision of the power and ingenuity of the mind of man. Busy boats chug and scurry about the river — racy speed boats, stolid, snorting tugs. If I had long days of sight ahead, I should spend many of them watching the delightful activity upon the river.

I look ahead, and before me rise the fantastic towers of New York, a city that seems to have stepped from the pages of a fairy story. What an awe-inspiring sight, these glittering spires, these vast banks of stone and steel — structures such as the gods might build for themselves! This animated picture is a part of the lives of millions of people every day. How many, I wonder, give it so much as a second glance? Very few, I fear. Their eyes are blind to this magnificent sight because it is so familiar to them.

I hurry to the top of one of those gigantic structures, the Empire State Building, for there, a short time ago, I "saw" the city below through the eyes of my secretary. I am anxious to compare my fancy with reality. I am sure I should not be disappointed in the panorama spread out before me, for to me it would be a vision of another world.

Now I begin my rounds of the city. First, I stand at a busy corner, merely looking at people, trying by sight of them to understand something of their lives. I see smiles, and I am happy. I see serious determination, and I am proud. I see suffering, and I am compassionate.

I stroll down Fifth Avenue. I throw my eyes out of focus, so that I see no particular object but only a seething kaleidoscope of color. I am certain that the colors of women's dresses moving in a throng must be a gorgeous spectacle of which I should never tire. But perhaps if I had sight I should be like most other women — too interested in styles and the cut of individual dresses to give much attention to the splendor of color in the mass. And I am convinced, too, that I should become an inveterate window shopper, for it must be a delight to the eye to view the myriad articles of beauty on display.

From Fifth Avenue I make a tour of the city — to Park Avenue, to the slums, to factories, to parks where children play. I take a stay-at-home trip abroad by visiting the foreign quarters. Always my eyes are open wide to all the sights of both happiness and misery so that I may probe deep and add to my understanding of how people work and live. My heart is full of the images of people and things. My eye passes lightly over no single trifle; it strives to touch and hold closely each thing its gaze rests upon. Some sights are pleasant, filling the heart with happiness; but some are miserably pathetic. To these latter I do not shut my eyes, for they, too, are part of life. To close the eye on them is to close the heart and mind.

My third day of sight is drawing to an end. Perhaps there are many serious pursuits to which I should devote the few remaining hours, but I am afraid that on the evening of that last day I should again run away to the theatre, to a hilariously funny play, so that I might appreciate the overtones of comedy in the human spirit.

At midnight my temporary respite from blindness would cease, and permanent night would close in on me again. Naturally in those three short days I should not have seen all I wanted to see. Only when darkness had again descended upon me should I realize how much I had left unseen. But my mind would be so crowded with glorious memories that I should have little time for regrets. Thereafter the touch of every object would bring a glowing memory of how that object looked.

Perhaps this short outline of how I should spend three days of sight does not agree with the programme you would set for yourself if you knew that you were about to be stricken blind. I am, however, sure that if you actually faced that fate your eyes would open to things you had never seen before, storing up memories for the long night ahead. You would use your eyes as never before. Everything you saw would become dear to you. Your eyes would touch and embrace every object that came within your range of vision. Then, at last, you would really see, and a new world of beauty would open itself before you.

I who am blind can give one hint to those who see — one admonition to those who would make full use of the gift of sight: Use your eyes as if tomorrow you would be stricken blind. And the same method can be applied to the other senses. Hear the music of voices, the song of a bird, the mighty strains of an orchestra, as if you would be stricken deaf tomorrow. Touch each object you want to touch as if tomorrow your tactile sense would fail. Smell the perfume of flowers, taste with relish each morsel, as if tomorrow you could never smell and taste again. Make the most of every sense; glory in all the facets of pleasure and beauty which the world reveals to you through the several means of contact which Nature provides. But of all the senses, I am sure that sight must be the most delightful.

我的成长日记

海伦·凯勒的书信是至关重要的，这些书信不仅是她生活故事的补充，还充分展示了她在思想和表达能力方面的成长过程，也正是这样的成长，使她出类拔萃。

这些信件之所以不一般，不仅是因为它们出自一个既失聪又失明的女孩之手，让我们充满好奇，而且还因为这些信件几乎从第一封起，本身也都写得很好。其中最好的是那些海伦·凯勒谈论她自己、用她的经历讲述她的世界的部分。

这些信件使海伦·凯勒的写作能力得到了极大的训练。她鹦鹉学舌似的重复，她对新词的有意展示，都令人感到欣喜并受到启发。通过写信，她向人们展示的不仅是她学到了什么，还有她是如何学习，如何让新知识和新词汇成为她自己的东西的。

此部分选录了她最具可读性和最具价值的部分信件。英文原文原封不动地保留了海伦·凯勒所写的全部内容，包括标点、拼写以及所有其他的东西。

一

快乐的铅笔

电话机的发明者贝尔博士也是一位致力于聋哑教育的慈善家。正是在他的帮助下，沙利文小姐来到了海伦的身畔。海伦毕生都很珍视这份最持久的友谊。

沙利文小姐1887年3月3日开始担任小海伦的家庭教师，8个月后，小海伦就能熟练地给家长、朋友写信。这封语言流畅，几乎没有语法错误的信正是写给贝尔博士的。

致亚历山大·格雷汉姆·贝尔博士

（塔斯坎比亚，1887年11月）

尊敬的贝尔先生，

我很高兴给您写信。父亲会寄相片给您。我和父亲和姑姑在华盛顿拜访了您。我还玩了您的手表。我很爱您。我在华盛顿看了医生。他看了我的眼睛。我能读我书里的故事。我可以写字、可以拼读、可以数数。好女孩。我妹妹会走会跑。我们和江博玩得很开心。普林斯不是一条好狗。他抓不到鸟。老鼠把乳鸽杀了。我很抱歉。老鼠不知道错。我和妈妈以及老师六月去波士顿。我会看到失明的小女孩们。南希要跟我一起

去。她是个很好的洋娃娃。爸爸会给我买可爱的新手表。安娜表姐送给我一个漂亮娃娃。她的名字叫艾莉。

再见

海伦·凯勒

To Dr. Alexander Graham Bell

(*Tuscumbia, November, 1887.*)

Dear Mr. Bell.

I am glad to write you a letter. Father will send you picture. I and Father and aunt did go to see you in Washington. I did play with your watch. I do love you. I saw doctor in Washington. He looked at my eyes. I can read stories in my book. I can write and spell and count. good girl. My sister can walk and run. we do have fun with Jumbo. Prince is not good dog. He can not get birds. Rat did kill baby pigeons. I am sorry. Rat does not know wrong. I and mother and teacher will go to Boston in June. I will see little blind girls. Nancy will go with me. She is a good doll. Father will buy me lovely new watch. Cousin Anna gave me a pretty doll. Her name is Allie.

Good-by,

HELEN KELLER.

二

美妙的世界

到 1888 年年初，海伦能更加熟练地使用习语了。她的书信里出现了很多包括色彩词在内的形容词。虽然她不能看见那些缤纷的颜色，但聪慧的她学会了使用这些美丽的词汇，而且她的表达是那么的亲切真实。信中的阿纳戈诺斯先生是海伦即将就读的帕金斯学校的校长。

致迈克尔·阿纳戈诺斯先生

（亚拉巴马州塔斯坎比亚，1888 年 2 月 24 日）

我尊敬的阿纳戈诺斯先生，——我很高兴用盲文给您写信。今天早上吕西安·汤普森送给我一束漂亮的紫罗兰、番红花和黄水仙。星期天艾德琳·摩西给我买了一个可爱的洋娃娃。它来自纽约。她的名字叫艾德琳·凯勒。她会闭眼、弯手臂、坐下、站直。她穿着一套红色的衣服。她是南希的妹妹，我是她们的妈妈。艾莉是她们的表妹。南希是个坏小孩，我去孟菲斯的时候她大声哭，我用棍子打了她。

米尔德丽德用面包屑喂小鸡。我喜欢跟小妹妹玩。

我和老师去孟菲斯看望南妮姨妈和奶奶。路易斯是南妮姨妈的孩子。老师给我买了漂亮的衣服、手套、长袜和假领子，奶奶给我做了暖和的法兰绒衣服，南妮姨妈给我做了围裙。女士给我做了漂亮的帽子。我去看了

罗伯特、格雷夫斯先生、格雷夫斯夫人、小纳塔利、法拉斯先生、马约先生、玛丽还有其他人。我很爱罗伯特和老师。她让我今天不要再写了。我累了。

我在格雷夫斯先生的口袋里发现了一盒糖。爸爸带我们去看蒸汽船,它就像房子。船在很大的河上。耶茨今天翻整了院子种草。骡子拉犁。妈妈要在园子里种蔬菜。爸爸要种瓜、豌豆和其他豆类。

表哥贝尔星期六要来看我们。妈妈要为晚餐准备冰激凌,我们晚餐可以吃冰激凌和蛋糕。吕西安·汤普森病了。我为他难过。

我和老师去院子里散了步,我知道了花和树是怎么生长的。太阳从东边升起,从西边落下。谢菲尔德在北方,塔斯坎比亚在南方。我们六月要去波士顿。我会跟失明的小女孩们玩得很好。

再见

海伦·凯勒

To Mr. Michael Anagnos

(*Tuscumbia, Ala., Feb. 24th, 1888.*)

My dear Mr. Anagnos, —I'm glad to write you a letter in Braille. This morning Lucien Thompson sent me a beautiful bouquet of violets and crocuses and jonquils. Sunday Adeline Moses brought me a lovely doll. It came from New York. Her name is Adeline Keller. She can shut her eyes and bend her arms and sit down and stand up straight. She has on a pretty red dress. She is Nancy's sister and I am their mother. Allie is their cousin. Nancy was a bad child when I went to Memphis she cried loud, I whipped her with a stick.

Mildred does feed little chickens with crumbs. I love to play with little sister.

Teacher and I went to Memphis to see aunt Nannie and grandmother. Louise is aunt Nannie's child. Teacher bought me a lovely new dress and gloves and stockings and collars and grandmother made me warm flannels, and aunt Nannie made me aprons. Lady made me a pretty cap. I went to see Robert and

Mr. Graves and Mrs. Graves and little Natalie, and Mr. Farris and Mr. Mayo and Mary and everyone. I do love Robert and teacher. She does not want me to write more today. I feel tired.

I found box of candy in Mr. Graves's pocket. Father took us to see steam boat it is like house. Boat was on very large river. Yates plowed yard today to plant grass. Mule pulled plow. Mother will make garden of vegetables. Father will plant melons and peas and beans.

Cousin Bell will come to see us Saturday. Mother will make ice-cream for dinner, we will have ice-cream and cake for dinner. Lucien Thompson is sick. I am sorry for him.

Teacher and I went to walk in the yard, and I learned about how flowers and trees grow. Sun rises in the east and sets in the west. Sheffield is north and Tuscumbia is south. We will go to Boston in June. I will have fun with little blind girls.

Good bye

HELEN KELLER.

"莫里叔叔"是指美国肯塔基州诺曼底的莫里森·黑迪先生,他在小时候便失明和失聪。他平生创作了一些令人喜爱的诗篇。小海伦喜爱并崇拜着他。

致莫里森·黑迪先生

(亚拉巴马州塔斯坎比亚,1888年3月1日)

我亲爱的莫里叔叔——我很高兴给您写这封信,我很爱您,见到您时我会拥抱并亲吻您。

星期一阿纳戈诺斯先生会来看我。我非常喜欢和罗伯特在温暖明媚

的阳光下跳跃、奔跑。我认识了住在肯塔基州列克星敦市的小女孩。她的名字叫凯瑟琳·霍布森。

6月份妈妈和老师会陪伴我去波士顿，我将和那里的失明的小女孩度过一段愉快的时光，黑尔先生会送我漂亮的故事书，我在书中能读到有关狮子、老虎和熊的故事。

米尔德丽德不能去波士顿，她哭了。我喜欢跟小妹妹一起玩，她是个柔弱的小宝宝。伊娃的身体要好些。

耶茨把蚂蚁弄死了，因为耶茨在花园里挖洞，蚂蚁咬了他。阿纳戈诺斯先生看到了橘子，它们像金色的苹果。

星期天太阳照耀大地的时候，罗伯特会来看我，我们将一起玩耍。我的堂兄弗兰克住在路易斯维尔。我又要去孟菲斯拜访法瑞斯先生、格雷夫斯夫人、梅尔先生和格雷夫斯先生。娜塔莉是个好女孩，从来不哭，她会长大的，格雷夫斯夫人正在给她做短裙。娜塔莉有辆小马车。梅尔先生去了杜克山，带回了芬芳可爱的花朵。

爱您、吻您！

海伦·A. 凯勒

To Mr. Morrison Heady

(*Tuscumbia, Ala., March 1st 1888.*)

My dear uncle Morrie, —I am happy to write you a letter, I do love you, and I will hug and kiss you when I see you.

Mr. Anagnos is coming to see me Monday. I do love to run and hop and skip with Robert in bright warm sun. I do know little girl in Lexington Ky. her name is Katherine Hobson.

I am going to Boston in June with mother and teacher, I will have fun with little blind girls, and Mr. Hale will send me pretty story. I do read stories in my book about lions and tigers and bears.

Mildred will not go to Boston, she does cry. I love to play with little sister, she is weak and small baby. Eva is better.

Yates killed ants, ants stung Yates. Yates is digging in garden. Mr. Anagnos did see oranges, they look like golden apples.

Robert will come to see me Sunday when sun shines and I will have fun with him. My cousin Frank lives in Louisville. I will come to Memphis again to see Mr. Farris and Mrs. Graves and Mr. Mayo and Mr. Graves. Natalie is a good girl and does not cry, and she will be big and Mrs. Graves is making short dresses for her. Natalie has a little carriage. Mr. Mayo has been to Duck Hill and he brought sweet flowers home.

With much love and a kiss

HELEN A. KELLER.

5月底，凯勒夫人和沙利文小姐带小海伦去波士顿。途中，她们在华盛顿逗留数日，拜访了和小海伦通过信的亚历山大·格雷汉姆·贝尔博士，并受到克利夫兰总统（Stephen Grover Cleveland）的接见。5月26日，她们抵达波士顿，造访了帕金斯学校，在那里海伦见到了一年前和她通过信的失明女孩们。

7月初，小海伦在马萨诸塞州的布鲁斯特度过了整个夏天。她平生第一次"看到"大海，非常激动，后来她曾多次提及此事。

致玛丽·C.摩尔小姐

（马萨诸塞州南波士顿，1888年9月）

我亲爱的摩尔小姐：

当您收到可爱的小朋友的来信时会高兴吗？您是我的朋友，我真爱您。我的宝贝小妹妹很好。她喜欢坐在我的小摇椅上，拍着她的小猫咪睡觉。

您想见到可爱的米尔德丽德吗？她是个漂亮宝贝。她的眼睛又大又蓝；脸颊柔软而圆润、红得像玫瑰；头发亮亮的、泛着金色。她不大声哭的时候很甜美可爱。明年夏天米尔德丽德就可以和我一起到花园里摘又大又甜的草莓了，她会很高兴的。我希望她不要吃太多美味的水果，那样她会生病的。

您有空的时候会来亚拉巴马州看我吗？我的叔叔詹姆斯要给我买一匹温顺的小马驹和一辆漂亮的小马车，如果能带着您和哈里去兜风，我会十分开心的。我希望哈里不要害怕我的小马驹。我想我父亲有一天会给我买个漂亮的弟弟回来。我会对我的小弟弟很温柔、很有耐心的。当我去那些陌生的国度参观旅行时，我的弟弟和米尔德丽德会跟我的奶奶待在一起，他们太小，不能见那么多的人，我想他们在风大浪急的大海上会号啕大哭的。

等贝克船长康复后，他会用大船带我去非洲。我会看到狮子、老虎和猴子。我会带一只小狮子、一只白猴子和一只温顺的熊回家。我在布鲁斯特度过了一段美好时光。我几乎每天都去游泳，我和卡莉、弗兰克、小海伦玩得很高兴。我们在深水里互相嬉戏、玩闹。我现在不怕在水上漂浮了。哈里能漂浮在水上游泳吗？上星期四我们到了波士顿，阿纳戈诺斯先生很高兴见到我，他拥抱并亲吻我。小女孩们下星期三会回学校。

您可以告诉哈里给我写封长信吗？你们来塔斯坎比亚看我时，我希望爸爸会给你们好多的甜苹果、多汁的桃子、漂亮的梨、美味的葡萄和大西瓜。

我希望您想着我、爱我，因为我是个很好的小孩。

爱您，送上两个吻。

来自您的小朋友

海伦·A. 凯勒

To Miss Mary C. Moore

(*So. Boston, Mass. Sept 1888*)

My dear Miss Moore

Are you very glad to receive a nice letter from your darling little friend? I love you very dearly because you are my friend. My precious little sister is quite well now. She likes to sit in my little rocking-chair and put her kitty to sleep. Would you like to see darling little Mildred? She is a very pretty baby. Her eyes are very big and blue, and her cheeks are soft and round and rosy and her hair is very bright and golden. She is very good and sweet when she does not cry loud. Next summer Mildred will go out in the garden with me and pick the big sweet strawberries and then she will be very happy. I hope she will not eat too many of the delicious fruit for they will make her very ill.

Sometime will you please come to Alabama and visit me? My uncle James is going to buy me a very gentle pony and a pretty cart and I shall be very happy to take you and Harry to ride. I hope Harry will not be afraid of my pony. I think my father will buy me a beautiful little brother some day. I shall be very gentle and patient to my new little brother. When I visit many strange countries my brother and Mildred will stay with grandmother because they will be too small to see a great many people and I think they would cry loud on the great rough ocean.

When Capt. Baker gets well he will take me in his big ship to Africa. Then I shall see lions and tigers and monkeys. I will get a baby lion and a white monkey and a mild bear to bring home. I had a very pleasant time at Brewster. I went in bathing almost every day and Carrie and Frank and little Helen and I had fun. We splashed and jumped and waded in the deep water. I am not afraid to float now. Can Harry float and swim? We came to Boston last Thursday, and Mr. Anagnos was delighted to see me, and he hugged and kissed me. The little girls are coming back to school next Wednesday.

Will you please tell Harry to write me a very long letter soon? When you come to Tuscumbia to see me I hope my father will have many sweet apples and juicy peaches and fine pears and delicious grapes and large water melons.

I hope you think about me and love me because I am a good little child.

With much love and two kisses

From your little friend

HELEN A. KELLER.

8岁的小海伦像所有的孩童一样天真无邪,但她与生俱来的好奇心使她比普通孩子的视野更加开阔,思想也远比一般的孩子成熟得多。在以下这封信中小海伦以一颗博爱、宽广的心谈到了中国。

致凯特·亚当斯·凯勒夫人

（马萨诸塞州南波士顿,1888年9月24日）

亲爱的妈妈:

我想您会乐于知道我在西牛顿的一切情况。我和老师还有很多好朋友度过了愉快的时光。西牛顿离波士顿不远,我们坐蒸汽汽车很快就到了。

弗里曼夫人、卡莉、埃塞尔、弗兰克和海伦乘着一张巨大的四轮马车来车站接我们。我很高兴见到我的小朋友们,我拥抱并亲吻了他们。然后我们花了好长时间坐着马车看了西牛顿的所有美丽风景。许多漂亮的房子,周围有又大又软的绿草坪,有树木、鲜艳的花朵和喷泉。拉车的马叫"王子",它很温顺,喜欢疾驰。我们回到家,看到八只兔子、两只胖胖的小狗、一匹白色的漂亮小马驹、两只小猫咪和一只叫"唐"的卷毛狗。小马驹的名字叫"莫莉",我好好地骑了她一回;我不害怕,我希望我的叔叔快点帮我把可爱的小马驹和小马车一起买回来。

克里弗顿没有亲吻我,因为他不喜欢亲小女孩。他很害羞。我很高兴弗兰克、克拉伦斯、洛比、艾迪、查尔斯和乔治他们都不怎么害羞。我和许多小女孩玩得很高兴。我骑着卡莉的三轮车,采花、吃水果、跳来跳去、舞着、骑着。许多女士、先生们看着我们。露西、多拉和查尔斯出生在中国，我出生在美国，阿纳戈诺斯先生出生在希腊。德鲁先生说中国的小女孩不会用手指"讲话"，我想等我去中国我会教她们。有个中国保姆来看我，她的名字叫"阿苏"。她给我看中国有钱小姐穿的鞋，很小，因为她们的脚被裹过永远长不大。"阿妈"的意思是保姆。因为是星期天，蒸汽汽车不运行，我们只有坐马车回家。列车员和司机都很累回家休息去了。我在车上看到小威利·斯旺了，他给了我一个多汁的梨。他六岁了。我六岁的时候在做什么？您会让爸爸坐火车来看我和老师吗？伊娃和贝希病了，我很难过。我希望有一个愉快的生日聚会。我想让卡莉、埃塞尔、弗兰克、海伦来阿拉巴马看我。我回家后，米尔德丽德会和我一起睡觉吗？

爱您，送上一千个吻。

来自您可爱的小女儿。

海伦·A. 凯勒

To Mrs. Kate Adams Keller

(*So. Boston, Mass, Sept. 24th 1888.*)

My dear Mother,

　　I think you will be very glad to know all about my visit to West Newton. Teacher and I had a lovely time with many kind friends. West Newton is not far from Boston and we went there in the steam cars very quickly.

　　Mrs. Freeman and Carrie and Ethel and Frank and Helen came to station to meet us in a huge carriage. I was delighted to see my dear little friends and I hugged and kissed them. Then we rode for a long time to see all the beautiful things in West Newton. Many very handsome houses and large soft green lawns around them and trees and bright flowers and fountains. The horse's name was Prince and he was gentle and liked to trot very fast. When we went home we saw eight rabbits and two fat puppies, and a nice little white pony, and two wee kittens and a pretty curly dog named Don. Pony's name was Mollie and I had a nice ride on her back; I was not afraid, I hope my uncle will get me a dear little pony and a little cart very soon.

  Clifton did not kiss me because he does not like to kiss little girls. He is shy. I am very glad that Frank and Clarence and Robbie and Eddie and Charles and George were not very shy. I played with many little girls and we had fun. I rode on Carrie's tricicle and picked flowers and ate fruit and hopped and skipped and danced and went to ride. Many ladies and gentlemen came to see us. Lucy and Dora and Charles were born in China. I was born in America, and Mr. Anagnos was born in Greece. Mr. Drew says little girls in China cannot talk on their fingers but I think when I go to China I will teach them. Chinese nurse came to see me, her name was Asu. She showed me a tiny atze that very rich ladies in China wear because their feet never grow large. Amah means a nurse. We came home in horse cars because it was Sunday and steam cars do not go often on Sunday. Conductors and engineers do get very tired and go home to rest. I saw little Willie Swan in the car and he gave me a juicy pear. He was six years old. What did I do when I was six years old? Will you please ask my father to come to train to meet teacher and me? I am very sorry that Eva and Bessie are sick. I hope I can have a nice party my birthday, and I do want Carrie and Ethel and Frank and Helen to come to Alabama to visit me. Will Mildred sleep with me when I come home.

  With much love and thousand kisses.

  From your dear little daughter.

  HELEN A. KELLER.

三

学习的乐趣

7月，小海伦参观了"美国的故乡"普利茅斯。这封信是三个月之后写的，从小海伦童话般的故事叙述中可见她对她的"第一堂历史课"记得多么清楚。

致莫里森·黑迪先生

（马萨诸塞州南波士顿，1888年10月1日）

我亲爱的莫里叔叔——我想您会很高兴收到可爱的小朋友海伦的来信。我很高兴写信给您，因为我想念您和爱您。在您送给我的书中，我读到了优美的故事，如《查尔斯和他的小船》《阿瑟和他的梦境》《罗莎和绵羊》等。

我一直坐在大船里，这船就像军舰一样气派。妈妈、老师、霍普金斯夫人、阿纳戈诺斯先生、罗德卡纳奇先生和许多其他朋友一起去普利茅斯看了很多古迹。下面我给您讲一个关于普利茅斯的小故事。

很久以前，英格兰住着许多好人，国王和他的朋友们对这些好人不友善、不礼貌，也没耐心，因为国王不喜欢臣民违抗他的命令。人们不喜欢和国王一起去教堂做礼拜，他们更喜欢自己建一些漂亮的小教堂。

国王很愤怒。那些好人感到很遗憾，他们说，他们要去一个陌生的国度，离开可爱的家和朋友，以及可恶的国王。这样，他们把所有东西

放进大箱子里，告别了家乡。我为他们感到难过，因为他们痛哭流涕。他们来到荷兰，但一个人都不认识。他们不懂荷兰语，不知道人们在交谈什么。但很快他们学会了一些荷兰语单词，可他们更喜欢自己的母语，他们不想让小男孩和小女孩忘记母语而学说可笑的荷兰语。所以他们说，他们一定要去一个遥远的新国度，在那里建学校、房子、教堂和新城市。所以他们把所有东西放到大箱子里，跟他们的新朋友告别，驾驶大船寻找新国家。可怜的人们闷闷不乐，心里充满悲伤，因为他们对美洲不了解。我想小孩会害怕大海，因为大海足够强大，摇动大船，小孩会摔倒，撞到头。他们一连几个星期在大海上航行，看不到树、花和草，周围只有海水、美丽的天空，船行走得不快，因为他们对发动机和蒸汽机也不太了解。有一天，一个小男婴在船上出生了。他叫佩里格林·怀特。很遗憾的是，可怜的小佩里格林后来死了。人们每天都到甲板上寻找陆地的踪影。一天，船上发出了叫喊声，因为人们看到了陆地，心里激动万分，他们终于安全到达了新大陆。小女孩和小男孩们拍着巴掌跳起来。当他们踏上一块巨大的岩石时，大家高兴极了。我在普利茅斯看到了那块岩石、像"五月花"号一样的小船、可爱的小佩里格林睡过的摇篮，还有好多"五月花"号上的东西。您想来普利茅斯看看那些老物件吗？

我现在很累，我要去休息了。

我很爱您，送上许多吻。来自您的小朋友。

海伦·A.凯勒

To Mr. Morrison Heady

(*South Boston, Mass. October 1st, 1888.*)

My dear uncle Morrie, — I think you will be very glad to receive a letter from your dear little friend Helen. I am very happy to write to you because I think of you and love you. I read pretty stories in the book you sent me, about Charles and his boat, and Arthur and his dream, and Rosa and the sheep.

I have been in a large boat. It was like a ship. Mother and teacher and Mrs. Hopkins and Mr. Anagnos and Mr. Rodocanachi and many other friends went to Plymouth to see many old things. I will tell you a little story about Plymouth.

Many years ago there lived in England many good people, but the king and his friends were not kind and gentle and patient with good people, because the king did not like to have the people disobey him. People did not like to go to church with the king; but they did like to build very nice little churches for themselves.

The king was very angry with the people and they were sorry and they said, we will go away to a strange country to live and leave very dear home and friends and naughty king. So, they put all their things into big boxes, and said, Good-bye. I am sorry for them because they cried much. When they went to Holland they did not know anyone; and they could not know what the people were talking about because they did not know Dutch. But soon they learned some Dutch words; but they loved their own language and they did not want little boys and girls to forget it and learn to talk funny Dutch. So they said, We must go to a new country far away and build schools and houses and churches and make new cities. So they put all their things in boxes and said, Good-bye to their new friends and sailed away in a large boat to find a new country. Poor people were not happy for their hearts were full of sad thoughts because they did not know much about America. I think little children must have been afraid of a great ocean for it is very strong and it makes a large boat rock and then the little children would fall down and hurt their heads. After they had been many weeks on the deep ocean where they could not see trees or flowers or grass, but just water and the beautiful sky, for ships could not sail quickly then because men did not know about engines and steam. One day a dear little baby-boy was born. His name was Peregrine White. I am very sorry that poor little Peregrine is dead now. Every day the people went upon deck to look out for land. One day there was a great shout on the ship for the people saw the land and they were full of joy because they had reached a new country safely. Little girls and boys jumped and clapped their hands. They were all glad when they stepped upon a huge rock. I did see the rock in Plymouth and a little ship like the Mayflower and the cradle that dear little Peregrine slept in and many other things that came in the Mayflower. Would you like to visit Plymouth some time and see many old things.

Now I am very tired and I will rest.

With much love and many kisses, from your little friend.

HELEN A. KELLER.

下面这封信里出现了多国语言词汇，早在几个月求知欲旺盛的小海伦就开始学习外语。她不断吸收、消化这些词汇，还尝试运用它们，有时用得很巧妙，有时也像鹦鹉学舌。即使她不太懂这些词的意思，她也愿意把它们记下来。正是用这种方式，她学会了它们的正确发音，并用它们表达个人体验之外的思想。

致迈克尔·阿纳戈诺斯先生

（马萨诸塞州罗克斯伯里，1888年10月17日）

Mon cher Monsieur Anagnos,（亲爱的阿纳戈诺斯先生：）

我正坐在窗边，美丽的阳光照耀着我。昨天老师和我去了幼儿园。幼儿园有27个小孩，他们都是盲童。我很遗憾他们看不到东西。有一天他们会有好的视力吗？可怜的伊迪丝又盲又聋又哑。您对伊迪丝和我感到难过吗？我不久就回家看望妈妈、爸爸和我可爱的小妹妹。我希望您能来阿拉巴马看我，我会带您去坐我的小马车，我想您会喜欢看到我坐在小马驹背上的样子。我会戴上我可爱的帽子，穿上新的骑士服。如果阳光灿烂，我会带您去看雷拉、伊娃和贝希。当我满十三岁时，我会去好多陌生而美丽的国家旅行。我要去挪威爬高山、看冰雪。我希望不会摔倒，磕到头。我还要去英格兰拜访小少爷方特罗伊，他会很高兴带我参观他宏伟壮观的古堡。我们会追逐野鹿、喂兔子和捉松鼠。我不怕方特罗伊的大狗"道格"。我希望方特罗伊能带我去见一见仁慈的女王。我到法国会说法语。一个法国小男孩说：Parlez-vous Francais？（您会说法语吗？）我会说：Oui, Monsieur, vous avez un joli chapeau. Donnez moi un baiser.（会说，先生，您的帽子很漂亮，吻我一下。）我希望您能跟我去雅典看"雅典女郎"。她是一位可爱的女士，我将用希腊语同她交谈，我说：se agapo, pos echete，我想她会说：kalos，我说：chaere。您快点来看我，带我去剧院，好吗？当您来时，我会说：Kale emera，您回家时，我说：Kale nykta。我现在太累了，不想写了，Je vous time. Au revoir.（不占用您的时间了。再见）

来自您亲爱的小朋友

海伦·A. 凯勒

To Mr. Michael Anagnos

(*Roxbury, Mass. Oct. 17th, 1888.*)

Mon cher Monsieur Anagnos,

I am sitting by the window and the beautiful sun is shining on me. Teacher and I came to the kindergarten yesterday. There are twenty seven little children here and they are all blind. I am sorry because they cannot see much. Sometime will they have very well eyes? Poor Edith is blind and deaf and dumb. Are you very sad for Edith and me? Soon I shall go home to see my mother and my father and my dear good and sweet little sister. I hope you will come to Alabama to visit me and I will take you to ride in my little cart and I think you will like to see me on my dear little pony's back. I shall wear my lovely cap and my new riding dress. If the sun shines brightly I will take you to see Leila and Eva and Bessie. When I am thirteen years old I am going to travel in many strange and beautiful countries. I shall climb very high mountains in Norway and see much ice and snow. I hope I will not fall and hurt my head I shall visit little Lord Fauntleroy in England and he will be glad to show me his grand and very ancient castle. And we will run with the deer and feed the rabbits and catch the squirrels. I shall not be afraid of Fauntleroy's great dog Dougal. I hope Fauntleroy take me to see a very kind queen. When I go to France I will take French. A little French boy will say, *Parlez-vous Francais*? and I will say, *Oui, Monsieur, vous avez un joli chapeau. Donnez moi un baiser.* I hope you will go with me to Athens to see the maid of Athens. She was very lovely lady and I will talk Greek to her. I will say, *se agapo* and, *pos echete* and I think she will say, *kalos*, and then I will say *chaere*. Will you please come to see me soon and take me to the theater? When you come I will say, *Kale emera*, and when you go home I will say, *Kale nykta*. Now I am too tired to write more. *Je vous time. Au revoir*

  From your darling little friend

  HELEN A. KELLER.

  小海伦所接受的家庭教育非常全面，除了语言、文学、历史，她还学习了生物、天文、化学等。有趣的是她似乎一开始就能运用优美的语言来阐述那些刚学习到的枯燥的科学常识。

致索菲亚·C.霍普金斯夫人

（亚拉巴马州塔斯坎比亚，1888年12月11日）

亲爱的霍普金斯夫人：

　　我刚喂完我可爱的小鸽子。这只小鸽子是我的表兄辛普森上个星期天给我的。我用老师的名字"安妮"给它取名。我的小狗吃完晚餐就去睡觉了。小兔子们也睡了。我很快也要上床了。老师在给她的朋友写信。妈妈、爸爸和他们的朋友去看大火炉了，火炉是用来炼铁的。铁矿是在地底下找到的，但铁矿石是不能直接用的，要先放到炉中提炼，取出杂质，剩下纯净的铁。等这一切完成后，铁才能制造出机车、炉子、茶壶和很多其他东西。

　　煤也是在地底下找到的。很久以前，人类还没有生活在地球上，参天大树、高大的草丛、巨型蕨类植物和美丽的花覆盖着大地。当树叶落下，树木倒下，水流和土壤覆盖了它们。更多的树长出来又倒下，被水流和土壤覆盖。经过几千年的挤压，树木变得像岩石一样坚硬，就可以供人们作燃料了。您能不能在煤中看到树叶、蕨类和树皮的影子？男人们到地底下把煤挖出来，用蒸汽汽车运到大城市里，卖给人们当燃料。当室外非常寒冷时，煤让人们感到温暖和幸福。

　　您现在感到孤独和悲伤吗？我希望您能来看我并待很长一段时间。

非常爱您的小朋友
海伦·A. 凯勒

To Mrs. Sophia C. Hopkins

(*Tuscumbia, Ala. Dec. 11th. 1888.*)

My dear Mrs. Hopkins: —

I have just fed my dear little pigeon. My brother Simpson gave it to me last Sunday. I named it Annie, for my teacher. My puppy has had his supper and gone to bed. My rabbits are sleeping, too; and very soon I shall go to bed. Teacher is writing letters to her friends. Mother and father and their friends have gone to see a huge furnace. The furnace is to make iron. The iron ore is found in the ground; but it cannot be used until it has been brought to the furnace and melted, and all the dirt taken out, and just the pure iron left. Then it is all ready to be manufactured into engines, stoves, kettles and many other things.

Coal is found in the ground, too. Many years ago, before people came to live on the earth, great trees and tall grasses and huge ferns and all the beautiful flowers covered the earth. When the leaves and the trees fell, the water and the soil covered them; and then more trees grew and fell also, and were buried under water and soil. After they had all been pressed together for many thousands of years, the wood grew very hard, like rock, and then it was all ready for people to burn. Can yon see leaves and ferns and bark on the coal? Men go down into the ground and dig out the coal, and steam-cars take it to the large cities, and sell it to people to burn, to make them warm and happy when it is cold out of doors.

Are you very lonely and sad now? I hope you will come to see me soon, and stay a long time.

With much love from your little friend

HELEN A. KELLER.

1888年的整个冬日，沙利文小姐和海伦都待在塔斯坎比亚的家里生活学习，成效显著。春天来临，海伦已经学会灵活运用惯用语了。在1889年5月以后的信件中，几乎很难发现有用词不当之处。9岁的她用词准确、自如，语句流畅。

致迈克尔·阿纳戈诺斯先生

（亚拉巴马州塔斯坎比亚，1889年5月18日）

亲爱的阿纳戈诺斯先生——您肯定想象不到昨天晚上接到您的来信时我有多高兴。我很遗憾您要远行。我们会很想念很想念您的。我愿意和您一起去参观美丽的城市。我在亨茨维尔见过布莱森博士，他告诉我他去过罗马、雅典、巴黎和伦敦。他还爬过瑞士的高山，参观过意大利和法国漂亮的教堂，看过许多古老的城堡。我希望您把参观过的城市写信描述给我。您到荷兰时请把我的问候带给可爱的薇荷敏娜公主。她是个可爱的小姑娘，等她长大后她会成为荷兰女王。如果您去罗马尼亚，请向善良的伊丽莎白女王问候她的残疾小弟弟，告诉她我对她可爱的小女儿的去世深感悲痛。我想给那不勒斯的小王子维托奥一个吻，但老师说恐怕您记不住那么多留言。当我13岁时，我要亲自去拜访他们。

我和老师都很感谢您把方特罗伊小少爷的故事介绍给我们。

我很高兴今年夏天伊娃将和我待在一起。我们会过得很愉快的。请代我向霍华德问好，叫他回我信。星期四我们举行了野餐会，我们很喜欢在绿树成荫的树林里，大家对野餐很满意。

米尔德丽德正在院子里玩，妈妈在摘美味的草莓。爸爸和弗兰克叔叔去城里了。辛普森快回家了。米尔德丽德和我在亨茨维尔照了一些相片，我会送您一张。

玫瑰很美，妈妈种了很多漂亮的玫瑰花。"法兰西"和"拉马尔克"特别芬芳；"马芮夏尔·内尔""索夫特里""雅克米诺""妮菲尔特""里昂之星""贡提尔老爹""凯布瑞勒·德瑞维特"和"花园之珠"都是很美丽的玫瑰。

请代我向小男孩们和小女孩们问好。我每天都想他们，我打心底爱他们。当您从欧洲回来时，我希望您很好，并对回家感到高兴。别忘记代我问候卡里奥皮·凯哈伊雅小姐和弗朗西斯·德米特里尔斯·卡洛珀萨克斯先生。

您真诚的小朋友

海伦·亚当斯·凯勒

To Mr. Michael Anagnos

(*Tuscumbia, Ala., May 18, 1889.*)

My Dear Mr. Anagnos: —You cannot imagine how delighted I was to receive a letter from you last evening. I am very sorry that you are going so far away. We shall miss you very, very much. I would love to visit many beautiful cities with you. When I was in Huntsville I saw Dr. Bryson, and he told me that he had been to Rome and Athens and Paris and London. He had climbed the high mountains in Switzerland and visited beautiful churches in Italy and France, and he saw a great many ancient castles. I hope you will please write to me from all the cities you visit. When you go to Holland please give my love to the lovely princess Wilhelmina. She is a dear little girl, and when she is old enough she will be the queen of Holland. If you go to Romania please ask the good queen Elizabeth about her little invalid brother, and tell her that I am very sorry that her darling little girl died. I should like to send a kiss to Vittorio, the little prince of Naples, but teacher says she is afraid you will not remember so many messages. When I am thirteen years old I shall visit them all myself.

I thank you very much for the beautiful story about Lord Fauntleroy, and so does teacher.

I am so glad that Eva is coming to stay with me this summer. We will have fine times together. Give Howard my love, and tell him to answer my letter. Thursday we had a picnic. It was very pleasant out in the shady woods, and we all enjoyed the picnic very much.

Mildred is out in the yard playing, and mother is picking the delicious strawberries. Father and Uncle Frank are down town. Simpson is coming home soon. Mildred and I had our pictures taken while we were in Huntsville. I will send you one.

The roses have been beautiful. Mother has a great many fine roses. The

La France and the Lamarque are the most fragrant; but the Marechal Neil, Solfaterre, Jacqueminot, Nipheots, Etoile de Lyon, Papa Gontier, Gabrielle Drevet and the Perle des Jardines are all lovely roses.

　　Please give the little boys and girls my love. I think of them every day and I love them dearly in my heart. When you come home from Europe I hope you will be all well and very happy to get home again. Do not forget to give my love to Miss Calliope Kehayia and Mr. Francis Demetrios Kalopothakes.

　　Lovingly, your little friend,
　　HELEN ADAMS KELLER.

　　小海伦喜欢向朋友和亲人复述她"阅读"过的故事。以下这封写给她的法语老师的书信，她生动而传神地转述了她喜爱的一个童话故事。这封信显示了海伦早在幼年时期，就在写作和模仿方面具有较高的天赋。

致方妮·S.玛丽特小姐

（亚拉巴马州塔斯坎比亚，1889年5月17日）

　　亲爱的玛丽特小姐——我正在想一个可爱的小女孩，她哭得很伤心。她哭是因为她哥哥老取笑她。我告诉您她哥哥做了什么吧。我想您会为那个小孩感到遗憾的。她有一个别人给的特别漂亮的洋娃娃。哦，那是一个可爱又精致的洋娃娃！但是小女孩的哥哥，一个个子高高的小伙子，把洋娃娃拿走了，放在花园里的一棵高树上，然后跑开了。小女孩够不到洋娃娃，无法把洋娃娃弄下来，所以她哭了。洋娃娃也哭了，它的胳膊从绿色的树枝间伸出来，看起来很痛苦。很快，黑暗的夜晚来临了——难道整个晚上洋娃娃都得独自待在树上吗？这令小女孩简直无法忍受。"我要跟你待在一起"，她对洋娃娃说，虽然她也很胆小。她已经

清楚地看到几个戴着高高的尖帽子的小精灵，在阴暗的小径上跳舞，在树丛中偷看。它们越来越近，她把手伸向洋娃娃在的树上，精灵们哈哈大笑，对她指指点点。小女孩害怕极了，但是如果一个人没有做坏事的话，这些古怪的小精灵是不会伤害人的。"我做过错事吗？哦，是的！"小女孩说，"我曾经笑话过可怜的鸭子，它们用红破布裹着腿，蹒跚而行；笑话过可怜的动物，这是错误的！"

这是不是个可怜的故事？我希望她爸爸惩罚那个淘气的小男孩。下星期四您将见到我的老师，您高兴吗？她要回家休息，到秋天时，她会回来的。

您真诚的小朋友
海伦·凯勒

To Miss Fannie S. Marrett

(*Tuscumbia, Ala. May 17, 1889.*)

My Dear Miss Marrett—I am thinking about a dear little girl, who wept very hard. She wept because her brother teased her very much. I will tell you what he did, and I think you will feel very sorry for the little child. She had a most beautiful doll given her. Oh, it was a lovely and delicate doll! but the little girl's brother, a tall lad, had taken the doll, and set it up in a high tree in the garden, and had run away. The little girl could not reach the doll, and could not help it down, and therefore she cried. The doll cried, too, and stretched out its arms from among the green branches, and looked distressed. Soon the dismal night would come—and was the doll to sit up in the tree all night, and by herself? The little girl could not endure that thought. "I will stay with you," said she to the doll, although she was not at all courageous. Already she began to see quite plainly the little elves in their tall pointed hats, dancing down the dusky alleys, and peeping from between the bushes, and they seemed to come nearer and nearer; and she stretched her hands up towards the tree in which the doll sat and they laughed, and pointed their fingers at her. How terrified was the little girl; but if one has not done anything wrong, these strange little elves cannot harm one. "Have I done anything wrong? Ah, yes!" said the little girl. "I have laughed at the poor duck, with the red rag tied round its leg. It hobbled, and that made me laugh; but it is wrong to laugh at the poor animals!"

Is it not a pitiful story? I hope the father punished the naughty little boy. Shall you be very glad to see my teacher next Thursday? She is going home to rest, but she will come back to me next autumn.

Lovingly, your little friend,

HELEN KELLER.

这年夏天，沙利文小姐离开海伦近三个半月，这是她们师生之间的第一次分离。小海伦用这封长长的书信热情而诚挚地表达了她对老师的思念、盼望之情。此后，在她们接下来15年的亲密相伴中，仅有一次持续几天的短暂分开。

致安妮·曼斯菲尔德·沙利文小姐

（亚拉巴马州塔斯坎比亚，1889年8月7日）

最亲爱的老师——我很高兴今天晚上给您写信，因为一整天我都在想念您。我坐在走廊上，我的小白鸽栖息在我的椅子背后，看我写字。她的褐色小伙伴跟别的鸟飞走了；但安妮不悲伤，因为她喜欢跟我待在一起。方特罗伊在楼上睡着了，南希正在哄露西睡觉。也许模仿鸟[1]在唱安眠曲。

①模仿鸟：别名嘲鸫，分布于美国北部到整个巴西，体长23~25厘米，羽毛呈灰褐色，是食肉鸟。它的歌声悠扬，悦耳动听。许多音调是从别处模仿来的，如其他鸟的叫声，人声，甚至机器发出的声音。

美丽的鲜花也在怒放。空气里充满了茉莉花、天芥菜花和玫瑰花的芬芳。天气越来越热，所以爸爸8月20号要带我们去"采石场"避暑。我想我们会有一段在凉爽、宜人的森林里的美好日子。我会写信告诉您我们做的有趣的事。我很高兴莱斯特和亨利都是好孩子。代我给他们好多甜蜜的吻。

那个喜欢美丽星星的小男孩叫什么名字？伊娃给我讲了一个关于可爱的小女孩"海蒂"的故事。您会把故事书送给我吗？我想要台打字机。

小阿瑟长得很快。他现在穿上短童装了。莱拉表姐说他很快就会走路了。那时我牵着他柔软、圆胖的小手，在明媚的阳光下散步。他会摘最大的玫瑰，追逐最艳丽的蝴蝶。我会把他照顾得很好，不会让他摔倒、受伤。爸爸和几位绅士昨天去打猎。爸爸打了38只鸟。我们把其中一些做了晚餐，它们很好吃。上星期一辛普森打到一只美丽的鹤，鹤是又大又强壮的鸟。他的翅膀有我的手臂长，他的喙有我的脚大。他吃小鱼和其他小动物。爸爸说他可以整天飞而几乎不用停。

米尔德丽德是世界上最可爱、最甜美的小女孩了。她也很淘气。有时趁妈妈不注意，她会跑到葡萄园，在围裙里装满美味的葡萄。您回来时，我想她会用柔软的双臂紧紧搂着您、拥抱您。

星期天我去了教堂。我喜欢去教堂，因为可以见到我的朋友们。

一个绅士给了我一张漂亮的明信片。那是一个磨坊的照片，旁边还有一条美丽的小溪。水上有条小船飘着，芬芳的百合花在船边盛开。离磨坊不远处有所古老的房子，周围长满了树。屋顶有八只鸽子，台阶上有只大狗。"珍珠"现在是条骄傲的狗妈妈了。她生了八只小狗，并且她认为自己的小狗狗是世上最漂亮的。

我每天都读书。我很喜欢很喜欢读书。我希望您快点回来。我十分地想念您。我有好多事弄不明白，因为我亲爱的老师不在。给您五千个吻和我能表达的更多的爱。我要送给H夫人深深的爱和一个吻。

来自您深爱的小学生

海伦·A. 凯勒

To Miss Anne Mansfield Sullivan

(*Tuscumbia, Ala, August 7, 1889.*)

Dearest Teacher—I am very glad to write to you this evening, for I have been thinking much about you all day. I am sitting on the piazza, and my little white pigeon is perched on the back of my chair, watching me write. Her little brown mate has flown away with the other birds; but Annie is not sad, for she likes to stay with me. Fauntleroy is asleep upstairs, and Nancy is putting Lucy to bed. Perhaps the mocking bird is singing them to sleep. All the beautiful flowers are in bloom now. The air is sweet with the perfume of jasmines, heliotropes and roses. It is getting warm here now, so father is going to take us to the Quarry on the 20th of August. I think we shall have a beautiful time out in the cool, pleasant woods. I will write and tell you all the pleasant things we do. I am so glad that Lester and Henry are good little infants. Give them many sweet kisses for me.

What was the name of the little boy who fell in love with the beautiful star? Eva has been telling me a story about a lovely little girl named Heidi. Will you please send it to me? I shall be delighted to have a typewriter.

Little Arthur is growing very fast. He has on short dresses now. Cousin Leila thinks he will walk in a little while. Then I will take his soft chubby hand in mine, and go out in the bright sunshine with him. He will pull the largest roses, and chase the gayest butterflies. I will take very good care of him, and not let him fall and hurt himself. Father and some other gentlemen went hunting yesterday. Father killed thirty-eight birds. We had some of them for supper, and they were very nice. Last Monday Simpson shot a pretty crane. The crane is a large and strong bird. His wings are as long as my arm, and his bill is as long as my foot. He eats little fishes, and other small animals. Father says he can fly nearly all day without stopping.

Mildred is the dearest and sweetest little maiden in the world. She is very roguish, too. Sometimes, when mother does not know it, she goes out into the vineyard, and gets her apron full of delicious grapes. I think she would like to put her two soft arms around your neck and hug you.

Sunday I went to church. I love to go to church, because I like to see my friends.

A gentleman gave me a beautiful card. It was a picture of a mill, near a beautiful brook. There was a boat floating on the water, and the fragrant lilies were growing all around the boat. Not far from the mill there was all old house, with many trees growing close to it. There were eight pigeons on the roof of the house, and a great dog on the step. Pearl is a very proud mother-dog now. She has eight puppies, and she thinks there never were such fine puppies as hers.

I read in my books every day. I love them very, very, very much. I do want you to come back to me soon. I miss you so very, very much. I cannot know about many things, when my dear teacher is not here. I send you five thousand kisses, and more love than I can tell. I send Mrs. H. much love and a kiss.

From your affectionate little pupil,

HELEN A. KELLER.

1888年，8岁的海伦开始加入帕金斯学校学习。1889年秋天，经历漫长别离的海伦和沙利文小姐一起回到南波士顿的帕金斯学校。小海伦继续她已经完全适应的校园生活。

致米尔德丽德·凯勒小姐

（南波士顿，1889年10月24日）

我可爱的小妹妹——早上好！我会随信给你寄一份生日礼物。我希望它会给你带来快乐,因为我很高兴送给你这个礼物。裙子是蓝色的,像你的眼睛的颜色;糖果是甜的,就像可爱的你。我想妈妈会很高兴为你穿上新裙子的,你穿起来肯定漂亮得像玫瑰。图画书会告诉你许多奇特的野生动物的故事。你不要害怕它们。它们不会从图画中出来伤害你。

我每天都去上学,我学到了很多新东西。早上八点钟我学习算术,我喜欢它。九点我和小女孩们去体育馆,我们玩得很高兴。我希望你在这里,可以和三只小松鼠、两只温顺的鸽子玩,还可以为可爱的小知更鸟搭个漂亮的窝。模仿鸟不会生活在寒冷的北方。十点我学习我们所居住的地球的知识。十一点我和老师交谈,十二点我学习动物学。我还不知道下午干什么。

现在,我亲爱的小米尔德丽德,再见!代我向爸爸、妈妈问好,拥抱、亲吻他们。老师也向他们问好。

来自你亲爱的姐姐
海伦·A. 凯勒

To Miss Mildred Keller

(*South Boston, Oct. 24, 1889.*)

My Precious Little Sister: — Good Morning. I am going to send you a birthday gift with this letter. I hope it will please you very much, because it makes me happy to send it. The dress is blue like your eyes, and candy is sweet just like your dear little self. I think mother will be glad to make the dress for you, and when you wear it you will look as pretty as a rose. The picture-book will tell you all about many strange and wild animals. You must not be afraid of them. They cannot come out of the picture to harm you.

I go to school every day, and I learn many new things. At eight I study arithmetic. I like that. At nine I go to the gymnasium with the little girls and we have great fun. I wish you could be here to play three little squirrels, and two gentle doves, and to make a pretty nest for a dear little robin. The mocking bird does not live in the cold north. At ten I study about the earth on which we all live. At eleven I talk with teacher and at twelve I study zoölogy. I do not know what I shall do in the afternoon yet.

Now, my darling little Mildred, good bye. Give father and mother a great deal of love and many hugs and kisses for me. Teacher sends her love too.

From your loving sister,
HELEN A. KELLER.

下面这封信经美国诗人惠蒂尔之手标注过，原稿上有"海伦·A. 凯勒——聋哑且失明——九岁的年纪"笔迹字样。英文书信中"the browns"是笔误，是"棕色的眼睛"的意思。

致约翰·格林利夫·惠蒂尔

（马萨诸塞州南波士顿，盲人学校，1889年11月27日）

亲爱的诗人：

我想，当您收到一个您不认识的小姑娘的来信时，您会很惊讶；但是我想，当您听到我读您的诗篇感到非常愉快时，您一定又十分高兴。昨天我读了《校园时光》和《我的玩伴》，我特别喜欢。我很遗憾，那个有着"棕色眼睛"和"乱蓬蓬的金色鬈发"的可怜小女孩死了。生活在我们这个美丽的世界上是多么令人幸福呀！虽然我的眼睛看不到美丽的事物，但是我的内心能看到，我每一天都过得很快乐。

在花园里散步时，我无法看见美丽的花朵，但是我知道它们就在我周围，空气中不是散发着花朵的芳香吗？我还知道那种小小的吊钟花正在对伙伴们窃窃私语，否则它们就不会那样高兴了。我非常爱您，因为您教给我这么多有关花朵、鸟类和人类的事情。现在我必须说再见了，我希望您感恩节愉快。

来自您真诚的小朋友

海伦·A. 凯勒

To John Greenleaf Whittier

(*Inst. for the Blind, So. Boston, Mass., Nov. 27, 1889.*)

Dear Poet,

  I think you will be surprised to receive a letter from a little girl whom you do not know, but I thought you would be glad to hear that your beautiful poems make me very happy. Yesterday I read "In School Days" and "My Playmate," and I enjoyed them greatly. I was very sorry that the poor little girl with the browns and the "tangled golden curls" died. It is very pleasant to live here in our beautiful world. I cannot see the lovely things with my eyes, but my mind can see them all, and so I am joyful all the day long.

  When I walk out in my garden I cannot see the beautiful flowers but I know that they are all around me; for is not the air sweet with their fragrance? I know too that the tiny lily-bells are whispering pretty secrets to their companions else they would not look so happy. I love you very dearly, because you have taught me so many things about flowers, and birds, and people. Now I must say, good-bye. I hope [you] will enjoy the Thanksgiving very much.

  From your loving little friend,

  HELEN A. KELLER.

  惠蒂尔回复了上面的这封信，可惜回信已经难以查找。不过下面这封信，

可以给我们做一些参考。

致凯特·亚当斯·凯勒夫人

（马萨诸塞州南波士顿，1889年12月3日）

亲爱的妈妈：在这个美丽的早晨，您的小女儿很高兴给您写信。今天这里很冷，还下起了雨。昨天米斯伯爵夫人又来看我。她带给我一束美丽的紫罗兰。她的两个女儿分别叫紫罗兰和五月。伯爵说等下次来美国的时候，他很乐意去参观塔斯坎比亚。米斯伯爵夫人说她也想看看您的花，听一听模仿鸟的鸣唱。等我去英国时，他们想让我去看望他们，并待上几个星期。他们还要带我去拜见女王。

我已经收到了诗人惠蒂尔的来信。他喜欢我。韦德先生希望我和老师来年春天去看望他。我们去吗？他说您必须亲自喂"雌狮"，因为如果她不跟其他狗在一起吃食，她就会变得更温顺。

威尔逊先生星期四来看望我们。我很高兴收到家里寄来的花。花送来的时候我们正在吃早餐，我的朋友们也和我一样喜欢这些花。感恩节② 那天我们吃了一顿丰盛的晚餐——火鸡和李子布丁。上星期我去参观了一个漂亮的艺术品商店，我看到了很多雕像，有位先生还送给了我一个天使。

在星期天，我登上一艘大军舰，并在上面做礼拜。礼拜结束后，水手们还带我们参观了军舰。船上一共有460名水手，他们对我很友好。有位水手还把我抱起来，这样我的脚就不会碰到水了。他们都穿着蓝色制服，戴着奇特的小帽子。星期四这里还发生了可怕的火灾。很多商店着了火，四个人被烧死了。我为他们感到遗憾。请告诉爸爸，让他给我写信。可爱的小妹妹怎么样了？请代我亲亲她。我必须停笔了。您亲爱的孩子送给您许多的爱。

海伦·A. 凯勒

②感恩节：美国和加拿大等国家的节日，由美国首创。自1941年起，感恩节定在每年11月的第四个星期四。

To Mrs. Kate Adams Keller

(*South Boston, Mass., Dec. 3, 1889.*)

My Dear Mother:—Your little danghter is very happy to write to you this beautiful morning. It is cold and rainy here today. Yesterday the Countess of Meath came again to see me. She gave me a beautiful bunch of violets. Her little girls are named Violet and May. The Earl said he should be delighted to visit Tuscumbia the next time he conies to America. Lady Meath said she would like to see your flowers, and hear the mocking birds sing. When I visit England they want me to come to see them, and stay a few weeks. They will take me to see the Queen.

I had a lovely letter from the poet Whittier. He loves me. Mr. Wade wants teacher and me to come and see him next spring. May we go? He said you must feed Lioness from your hand, because she will be more gentle if she does not eat with other dogs.

Mr. Wilson came to call on us one Thursday. I was delighted to receive the flowers from home. They came while we were eating breakfast, and my friends enjoyed them with me. We had a very nice dinner on Thanksgiving day—turkey and plum-pudding. Last week I visited a beautiful art store. I saw a great many statues, and the gentleman gave me an angel.

Sunday I went to church on board a great warship. After the services were over the soldier-sailors showed us around. There were four hundred and sixty sailors. They were very kind to me. One carried me in his arms so that my feet would not touch the water. They wore blue uniforms and queer little caps. There was a terrible fire Thursday. Many stores were burned, and four men were killed. I am very sorry for them. Tell father, please, to write to me. How is dear little sister? Give her many kisses for me. Now I must close. With much love, from your darling child,

HELEN A. KELLER.

海伦拜访美国诗人霍姆斯博士后,马上寄去她写给他的第一封信。不久之后,霍姆斯博士将此信收入他的餐桌漫谈(Table-talk)系列之《超越茶杯》(Over the Teacups)一书。

致奥利弗·温德尔·霍姆斯博士

(马萨诸塞州南波士顿,1890年3月1日)

和蔼可亲的诗人:自从在那个阳光明媚的星期天同您道别后,我多次想起您;我要给您写一封信,因为我爱您。我很遗憾有时没有小孩跟您一起玩,不过我想您会很高兴跟您的书在一起的,您还有很多很多朋友。在华盛顿诞辰纪念日那天,有许多人来这里看望盲童;我为他们朗诵您写的诗,还给他们看了一些美丽的贝壳,这些贝壳来自帕洛斯附近的一个小岛。

我正在读一个非常悲伤的故事,叫《小杰基》。杰基是个您能想象得到的最可爱的小家伙,但他又穷又盲。我经常想——在我小时候,识字之前——我觉得每个人都很快乐。当我开始了解巨大的痛苦时,我会感到很悲哀。但我现在明白了,如果世上只有欢乐,那么我们就永远都不能学会勇敢和有耐心。

我正在学习动物学中有关昆虫的知识,我已经了解到了蝴蝶的很多习性。它们不会像蜜蜂那样为我们酿蜜,但它们就像它们停歇的花朵一样美丽,它们总会给小孩子们带来欣喜。它们过着快乐的生活,一边在花朵间翩翩起舞,一边吮吸着花蜜,从不考虑明天。它们就像忘掉书本和学习的小男孩和小女孩一样,跑过森林和田野,采集野花,或跑进水塘去寻找芬芳的百合花,在灿烂的阳光下快乐无比。

如果我的小妹妹六月份来波士顿,您能让我带她去看您吗?她是一个可爱的小宝贝,我想您一定会喜欢她的。

现在我必须要对我那和蔼的诗人说再见了，因为在上床睡觉前，我还要给家人写一封信。

来自您真诚的小朋友

海伦·A. 凯勒

To Dr. Oliver Wendell Holmes

(*South Boston, Mass., March 1, 1890.*)

Dear, Kind Poet: —I have thought of you many times since that bright Sunday when I bade you good-bye; and I am going to write you a letter, because I love you. I am sorry that you have no little children to play with you sometimes; but I think you are very happy with your books, and your many, many friends. On Washington's birthday a great many people came here to see the blind children; and I read for them from your poems, and showed them some beautiful shells, which came from a little island near Palos.

I am reading a very sad story, called "Little Jakey." Jakey was the sweetest little fellow you can imagine, but he was poor and blind. I used to think—When I was small, and before I could read—that everybody was always happy, and at first it made me very sad to know about pain and great sorrow; but now I know that we could never learn to be brave and patient, if there were only joy in the world.

I am studying about insects in zoology, and I have learned many things about butterflies. They do not make honey for us, like the bees, but many of them are as beautiful as the flowers they light upon, and they always delight the hearts of little children. They live a gay life, flitting from flower to flower, sipping the drops of honeydew, without a thought for the morrow. They are just like little boys and girls when they forget books and studies, and run away to the woods and the fields, to gather wild flowers, or wade in the ponds for fragrant lilies, happy in the bright sunshine.

If my little sister comes to Boston next June, will you let me bring her to see you? She is a lovely baby, and I am sure you will love her.

Now I must tell my gentle poet good-bye, for I have a letter to write home before I go to bed.

From your loving little friend,

HELEN A. KELLER.

四

用嘴说话的快乐

1890年的春天，小海伦学会了用嘴而不仅是用手与旁人交流，她是多么的喜悦啊，所以急于将这份快乐与所有人分享。

致萨拉·富勒小姐

（马萨诸塞州南波士顿，1890年4月3日）

亲爱的富勒小姐：

在这个美丽的早晨，我心里充满欢乐，因为我学会了很多新词，我还能说好几个句子。昨天晚上我到院子里对着月亮说话。我说："哦！月亮，到我这里来吧！"您觉得迷人的月亮会为我能和她说话而高兴吗？但我妈妈肯定会特别高兴的。我几乎等不到六月份了，我急切地想跟妈妈还有我可爱的小妹妹讲讲话。以前米尔德丽德对我用手指拼写是不大懂的，现在她可以坐在我腿上，我会告诉她好多事情让她高兴，我们俩在一起总是特别快乐。您能让那么多人快乐，所以您自己也会很快乐吗？我觉得您很善良、有耐心，我由衷地爱您。星期二，老师告诉我您想知道我是如何想要开口说话的。我会告诉您一切的，因为我清楚地记得自己的想法。在我很小的时候，我整天坐在妈妈腿上，因为胆小，所以不愿意一个人独处。我总是把小手放在妈妈的脸上，当她和别人

讲话时，我能感觉到她的脸部和嘴唇的移动，这让我觉得很有趣。我不知道她在做什么，因为我对任何事都一无所知。当我又大一点的时候，我学会了同保姆和黑人小伙伴一起玩耍，我注意到他们的嘴唇也像妈妈那样动，所以我也跟着动嘴唇。但有时我会很懊恼，就去重重地摸伙伴们的嘴。那时我还不知道这么做是很顽皮的举动。又过了很久，我亲爱的老师来到我身边，她教我用手指同别人交流，我感到既满足又高兴。但是当我来波士顿上学时，我遇到了一些聋人，他们也能像其他人一样用嘴交谈。有一天，一位曾去过挪威的女士来看我，她告诉我，她在那个遥远的国家看到过一个又盲又聋的小姑娘被教会说话，后来人们跟她讲话她就能听懂。这个好消息令我很兴奋，从那时起，我就确信我也能学会说话。我试图像我的小伙伴们那样发出声音，但是老师告诉我，声音是非常微妙、灵敏的，如果不能正确发音，就会造成伤害，老师承诺带我去见一位善良而聪慧的女士，她会教我正确地发音。那位女士就是您。现在我高兴得像一只小鸟，因为我可以说话了，也许我还能唱歌呢。我所有的朋友们都既吃惊又高兴。

您可爱的小学生
海伦·A. 凯勒

To Miss Sarah Fuller

(*South Boston, Mass., April 3, 1890*)

My dear Miss Fuller,

My heart is full of joy this beautiful morning, because I have learned to speak many new words, and I can make a few sentences. Last evening I went out in the yard and spoke to the moon. I said, "O! moon come to me!" Do you think the lovely moon was glad that I could speak to her? How glad my mother will be. I can hardly wait for June to come I am so eager to speak to her and to my precious little sister. Mildred could not understand me when I spelled with my fingers, but now she will sit in my lap and I will tell her many things to please her, and we shall be so happy together. Are you very, very happy because you can make so many people happy? I think you are very kind and patient. and I love you very dearly. My teacher told me Tuesday that you wanted to know how I came to wish to talk with my mouth. I will tell you all about it, for I remember my thoughts perfectly. When I was a very little child I used to sit in my mother's lap all the time, because I was very timid, and did not like to be left by myself. And I would keep my little hand on her face all the while, because it amused me to feel her face and lips move when she talked with people. I did not know then what she was doing, for I was quite ignorant of all things. Then when I was older I learned to play with my nurse and the little negro children and I noticed that they kept moving their lips just like my mother, so I moved mine too, but sometimes it made me angry and I would hold my playmates' mouths very hard. I did not know then that it was very naughty to do so. After a long time my dear teacher came to me, and taught me to communicate with my fingers and I was satisfied and happy. But when I came to school in Boston I met some deaf people who talked with their mouths like all other people, and one day a lady who had been to Norway came to see me, and told me of a blind and deaf girl she had seen in that far away land who had been taught to speak and understand others when they spoke to her. This good and happy news delighted me exceedingly, for then I was sure that I should learn also. I tried to make sounds like my little playmates, but teacher told me that the voice was very delicate and sensitive and that it would injure it to make incorrect sounds, and promised to take me to see a kind and wise lady who would teach me rightly. That lady was yourself. Now I am as happy as the little birds, because I can speak and perhaps I shall sing too. All of my friends will be so surprised and glad.

Your loving little pupil,

HELEN A. KELLER.

7月,帕金斯学校放暑假了,海伦和沙利文小姐回到了塔斯坎比亚。这是海伦学会"用嘴讲话"后第一次回家。

致菲利普斯·布鲁克斯先生

(亚拉巴马州塔斯坎比亚,1890年7月14日)

亲爱的布鲁克斯先生,我非常高兴在这个美丽的日子给您写信,因为您是我善良的朋友,我爱您,我还希望了解更多的事情。我已经在家待了三个星期了,而且,哦,能和亲爱的妈妈爸爸还有宝贝小妹妹在一件是多么高兴的事。我很难过和波士顿的朋友们分开了,但我急切地想见到我的小妹妹,几乎等不及火车把我带回家了。在老师面前,我必须要有耐心。和我刚去波士顿时相比,米尔德丽德长得更高更结实了,她是世界上最漂亮最可爱的小孩。我的父母听到我能讲话都很高兴,能带给他们这样一个惊喜让我开心极了。我想带给每个人欢乐是令人愉快的事。为什么亲爱的圣父会认为有时经历巨大的悲伤会对我们有好处?我一直都很快乐,小方特罗伊勋爵也很快乐,但可爱的小杰基的生活充满了悲伤。上帝没有把光明放进杰基的眼睛里,他看不见,而且他爸爸既无耐心也不爱他。您认为可怜的杰基是不是更爱圣父?因为他爸爸对他不好。上帝是怎样告诉人们他的家在天堂的?当人们做错事、伤害动物、对小孩不友善时,上帝就会伤心,但是他会教导人们具有同情心和爱心吗?我想他会告诉人们他是多么爱他们,他希望他们过得幸福愉快,而人们也不想让深爱着他们的圣父伤心,所以他们会做任何让圣父开心的事，他们爱每个人，友善待人，善待动物。

请跟我讲讲您所知道的有关上帝的事。我很想更多地了解慈爱的圣父，他既仁爱又睿智。我希望您抽时间给您的小朋友写信。要是今天能见到您该多好啊！现在波士顿的太阳很炙热吗？如果今天下午天气凉爽的话，我会带米尔德丽德骑我的驴子溜一溜。韦德先生把奈秋送给了我，他是一头您能想象得到的最漂亮的驴。在我们骑驴的时候，我的大狗雌狮会跟着我们，保护我们。昨天，我哥哥辛普森给我送了一些美丽的池塘百合——他真是我的好哥哥。

老师送给您最美好的回忆，爸爸和妈妈也送去他们的问候。

来自您真诚的小朋友

海伦·A. 凯勒

To Rev. Phillips Brooks

(*Tuscumbia, Alabama, July 14, 1890.*)

My dear Mr. Brooks, I am very glad to write to you this beautiful day because you are my kind friend and I love you, and because I wish to know many things. I have been at home three weeks, and Oh, how happy I have been with dear mother and father and precious little sister. I was very, very sad to part with all of my friends in Boston, but I was so eager to see my baby sister I could hardly wait for the train to take me home. But I tried very hard to be patient for teacher's sake. Mildred has grown much taller and stronger than she was when I went to Boston, and she is the sweetest and dearest little child in the world. My parents were delighted to hear me speak, and I was overjoyed to give them such a happy surprise. I think it is so pleasant to make everybody happy. Why does the dear Father in heaven think it best for us to have very great sorrow sometimes? I am always happy and so was Little Lord Fauntleroy, but dear Little Jakey's life was full of sadness. God did not put the light in Jakey's eyes and he was blind, and his father was not gentle and loving. Do you think poor Jakey loved his Father in heaven more because his other father was unkind to him? How did God tell people that his home was in heaven? When people do very wrong and hurt animals and treat children unkindly God is grieved, but what will he do to them to teach them to be pitiful and loving? I think he will tell them how dearly He loves them and that He wants them to be good and happy, and they will not wish to grieve their father who loves them so much, and they will want to please him in everything they do, so they will love each other and do good to everyone, and be kind to animals.

Please tell me something that you know about God. It makes me happy to know much about my loving Father, who is good and wise. I hope you will write to your little friend when you have time. I should like very much to see you to-day. Is the sun very hot in Boston now? this afternoon if it is cool enough I shall take Mildred for a ride on my donkey. Mr. Wade sent Neddy to me, and he is the prettiest donkey you can imagine. My great dog Lioness goes with us when we ride to protect us. Simpson, that is my brother, brought me some beautiful pond lilies yesterday—he is a very brother to me.

Teacher sends you her kind remembrances, and father and mother also send their regards.

From your loving little friend,
HELEN A. KELLER.

布鲁克斯博士的回信

（伦敦，1890年8月3日）

亲爱的海伦——我十分高兴收到你的来信。这封信跟着我穿过大洋，在这个宏伟的大都市中找到我，我会把我所知道的一切都告诉你，我也愿意花时间来写一封长信。什么时候你来波士顿，到我的书房来看看，如果你想听，我也会很愿意同你好好交流。

但是现在，我想对你说，我非常高兴看到你快乐，如此享受家庭生活。我确信，你和你爸爸妈妈、妹妹其乐融融的乡村生活，时常浮现在我的眼前。得知你很幸福，我也由衷地感到高兴。

尤其令我高兴的是，从你问的问题可以知道你的一些想法。当上帝对我们很好的时候，我们有没有考虑过上帝是怎么想的？让我告诉你我眼中的圣父是怎样的。我们每个人的内心都有爱的力量。爱在万物的灵魂中。如果没有爱的力量，生活就会很枯燥。我们都愿意这样想，阳光、风和树木会以它们自己的独特方式去爱，如果我们知道它们也有爱，我们也一定可以感受到它们的快乐。所以作为万物之灵的上帝是最伟大和最快乐的，也是最慈爱的。我们心中所有的爱都来自上帝，正如所有照耀花朵的光都来自太阳一样。我们爱得越多，我们就离上帝和他的大爱越近。

我想告诉你，因为你快乐，所以我也很快乐。这是真实的感受。所以这也是你的爸爸妈妈，还有你的老师和所有的朋友都会有的感受。你会不会想到因为你快乐，所以上帝也会感到快乐呀？我相信上帝一定是快乐的。他会比我们任何人更快乐，因为他比我们都要伟大，他不仅仅"看到"了你的快乐，而且他"制造"了快乐。当太阳把光明和色彩赐予玫瑰时，他就把快乐带给了你。我们之所以感到快乐，不仅仅是因为我们看到了朋友的欢乐，而且还因为我们带给了他们欢乐。难道我们不是这样做的吗？

但是上帝不仅仅希望我们"快乐"；他还希望我们"善良"，这是他

最希望的。他知道，只要我们心地善良，我们就能获得真正的快乐。世界上最大的烦恼是人们认为药物难以下咽，但是良药苦口利于病，药物会让我们恢复健康。我们会看到，好人也有可能陷入困境，这时我们就会想到耶稣所承受的世间最大的苦难，而这种苦难让他成为有大爱的人，我确信，他也是这个世界上从未见过的最快乐的人。

我很愿意同你谈论上帝。他会亲自告诉你爱的真谛。如果你请求他，他还会把爱放进你的心里。而耶稣是上帝的儿子，在上帝的所有子女中，他离上帝最近；他来到这个世界的目的，就是要告诉我们圣父的大爱。如果你读了他的话，你就会发现他的心里充满了上帝之爱。"我们知道上帝爱世人。"他说道。所以他自己也爱世人，虽然世人很残忍地对待他，并最终杀害了他。但他愿意为世人而死，因为他是那么爱世人。海伦，他依旧爱我们世人，他想告诉我们，我们也可以爱他。

所以说爱是一切。如果有人问你，或者你自问：上帝是什么？答案是这样的："上帝是爱。"这就是《圣经》给予我们的美好答案。

你所思考的这些问题，会随着你年龄的增长而逐渐明白。而现在要思考的，就是让你的每一次祈祷更虔诚，因为你亲爱的圣父把爱送给了你。

我希望你在我之后尽早返回波士顿，我会在九月中旬回来。我想听你讲所有的事情，别忘了说说那头驴。

问候你的爸爸、妈妈和老师。我希望能有机会见到你的小妹妹。

再见，亲爱的海伦。别忘了尽快给我写信，可把信直接寄到波士顿。

你真诚的朋友
菲利普斯·布鲁克斯

Dr. Brooks's Reply

(*London, August 3, 1890.*)

My Dear Helen—I was very glad indeed to get your letter. It has followed me across the ocean and found me in this magnificent great city which I should like to tell you all about if I could take time for it and make my letter long enough. Some time when you come and see me in my study in Boston I shall be glad to talk to you about it all if you care to hear.

But now I want to tell you how glad I am that you are so happy and enjoying your home so very much. I can almost think I see you with your father and mother and little sister, with all the brightness of the beautiful country about you, and it makes me very glad to know how glad you are.

I am glad also to know, from the questions which you ask me, what you are thinking about. I do not see how we can help thinking about God when He is so good to us all the time. Let me tell you how it seems to me that we come to know about our heavenly Father. It is from the power of love which is in our own hearts. Love is at the soul of everything. Whatever has not the power of loving must have a very dreary life indeed. We like to think that the sunshine and the winds and the trees are able to love in some way of their own, for it would make us know that they were happy if we know that they could love. And so God who is the greatest and happiest of all beings is the most loving too. All the love that is in our hearts comes from him, as all the light which is in the flowers comes from the sun. And the more we love the more near we are to God and His Love.

I told you that I was very happy because of your happiness. Indeed I am. So are your Father and your Mother and your Teacher and all your friends. But do you not think that God is happy too because you are happy? I am sure He is. And He is happier than any of us because He is greater than any of us, and also because He not merely *sees* your happiness as we do, but He also *made* it. He gives it to you as the sun gives light and color to the rose. And we are always most glad of what we not merely see our friends enjoy, but of what we give them to enjoy. Are we not?

But God does not only want us to be *happy*; He wants us to be *good*. He wants that most of all. He knows that we can be really happy only when we are good. A great deal of the trouble that is in the world is medicine which is very bad to take, but which it is good to take because it makes us better. We see how good people may be in great trouble when we think of Jesus who was the greatest sufferer that ever lived and yet was the best Being and so, I am sure, the happiest Being that the world has ever seen.

I love to tell you about God. But He will tell you Himself by the love which He will put into your heart if you ask Him. And Jesus, who is His Son, but is nearer to Him than all of us His other Children, came into the world on purpose to tell us all about our Father's Love. If you read His words, you will see how full His heart is of the love of God. "We *know* that He loves us," He says. He loved men Himself and though they were very cruel to Him and at last killed Him, He was willing to die for them because He loved them so. And, Helen, He loves men still, and He loves us, and He tells us that we may love Him.

And so love is everything. And if anybody asks you, or if you ask yourself what God is, answer, "God is Love." That is the beautiful answer which the Bible gives.

All this is what you are to think of and to understand more and more as you grow older, Think of it now, and let it make every blessing brighter because your dear Father sends it to you.

You will come back to Boston I hope soon after I do. I shall be there by the middle of September. I shall want you to tell me all about everything, and not forget the Donkey.

I send my kind remembrance to your father and mother, and to your teacher. I wish I could see your little sister.

Good Bye, dear Helen. Do write to me soon again, directing your letter to Boston.

Your affectionate friend
PHILLIPS BROOKS.

下面这封信是写给缅因州卡迪纳的某些绅士的，他们以海伦的名字命名了一艘从事国际木材运输的航船。

致布拉德斯特里特先生

（亚拉巴马州塔斯坎比亚，1890年7月14日）

我亲爱的善良朋友们：非常、非常感谢你们用我的名字给你们漂亮的新船命名。得知我在遥远的缅因州有那么多善良而可爱的好朋友，我感到非常高兴。当我在学习有关缅因州的森林知识时，无论如何也想象不到，一艘坚固而美丽的船正驶往世界各地，船上装着来自茂密森林的木材，那些遥远国家的人们就用这些木材建造可爱的家园、学校和教堂。我希望大海也能喜欢崭新的"海伦"号，并让她平稳地航行在蓝色的波浪上。请告诉那些在"海伦·凯勒"号上的勇敢水手们，待在家里的小海伦会常常怀着美好的祝愿想起他们的。我希望有一天能去拜访你们，并看看那跟我同名的漂亮的船。

送上我的爱，你们的小朋友
海伦·A. 凯勒

To Messrs. Bradstreet

(*Tuscumbia, Ala., July 14, 1890.*)

My Dear, Kind Friends: —I thank you very, very much for naming your beautiful new ship for me. It makes me very happy to know that I have kind and loving friends in the far-away State of Maine. I did not imagine, when I studied about the forests of Maine, that a strong and beautiful ship would go sailing all over the world, carrying wood from those rich forests, to build pleasant homes and schools and churches in distant countries. I hope the great ocean will love the new Helen, and let her sail over its blue waves peacefully. Please tell the brave sailors, who have charge of the HELEN KELLER, that little Helen who stays at home will often think of them with loving thoughts. I hope I shall see you and my beautiful namesake some time.

With much love, from your little friend,
HELEN A. KELLER.

海伦写给诗人惠蒂尔的信总带有一种诗意的雀跃,她崇拜这位诗人爷爷,写给他的信灵动、流畅,似一只轻巧飞翔的鸟。

致约翰·格林利夫·惠蒂尔

(南波士顿,1890年12月17日)

亲爱的诗人:

今天是您的生日,这是我今天早晨醒来时的第一个念头,我高兴地想,我要写封信告诉您,您的小朋友们非常爱您这位诗人和您的生日,今天晚上,他们要朗诵您的诗歌,并用音乐招待他们的朋友,以此来庆祝您的生日。我真希望那迅捷的爱之信使能在现场,以便把一些美妙的旋律传给您,传到您那位于梅里麦克河旁的小书房里。刚开始我很难过,因为太阳把它难璨的笑脸藏到乌云后面去了,但是后来我想到了原因,我又高兴了。原来太阳知道您喜欢看白雪皑皑的世界,所以它就把光芒都藏了起来,并让天空凝成小冰晶。等一切都准备好了以后,这些小冰晶就会轻轻地落下来,并温柔地覆盖在万物上。接着,太阳又会光芒万丈,让世界充满光明。如果我今天能和您在一起,那么我会送给您83个吻,每一个吻都代表您经历的一岁。对我来说,83年似乎很漫长。对您来说是不是也很长呢?我很想知道永恒是多少年。我恐怕自己想象不出那么长的时间。我收到了您夏天给我的来信,非常感谢您。现在,我正待在波士顿的盲人学校,但是我还没有开始上课,因为我最亲爱的朋友阿纳戈诺斯先生想让我休息一段时间,尽情地玩耍。

老师也挺好的,她要送给您亲切的问候。温馨的圣诞节就要来临了!我迫不及待地想开心一番!我祝愿您有一个非常快乐的圣诞节,我还祝您和每一个人在新年里充满欢欣和喜悦。

来自您的小朋友
海伦·A. 凯勒

To John Greenleaf Whittier

(*South Boston, Dec. 17, 1890.*)

Dear Kind Poet,

This is your birthday; that was the first thought which came into my mind when I awoke this morning; and it made me glad to think I could write you a letter and tell you how much your little friends love their sweet poet and his birthday. This evening they are going to entertain their friends with readings from your poems and music. I hope the swift winged messengers of love will be here to carry some of the sweet melody to you, in your little study by the Merrimac. At first I was very sorry when I found that the sun had hidden his shining face behind dull clouds, but afterwards I thought why he did it, and then I was happy. The sun knows that you like to see the world covered with beautiful white snow and so he kept back all his brightness, and let the little crystals form in the sky. When they are ready, they will softly fall and tenderly cover ever object. Then the sun will appear in all his radiance and fill the world with light. If I were with you to-day I would give you eighty-three kisses, one for each year you have lived. Eighty-three years seems very long to me. Does it seem long to you?I wonder how many years there will be in eternity. I am afraid I cannot think about so much time. I received the letter which you wrote to me last summer, and I thank you for it. I am staying in Boston now at the Institution for the Blind, but I have not commenced my studies yet, because my dearest friend, Mr Anagnos wants me to rest and play a great deal.

  Teacher is well and sends her kind remembrance to you. The happy Christmas time is almost here! I can hardly wait for the fun to begin! I hope your Christmas Day will be a very happy one and that the New Year will be full of brightness and joy for you and every one.

  From your little friend

  HELEN A. KELLER.

惠蒂尔的回信

  我亲爱的小朋友——我十分高兴在生日这天收到了这封令我愉快的信。我收到了两三百个朋友们的祝福，但你的祝福是最令我开心的。我一定会跟你讲一讲在欧克诺的日子的。当然，这里的太阳没有光芒，但我们在屋子里烧着木柴，屋子里弥漫着玫瑰和其他花卉的芳香，这些花都是远方的朋友们送给我的；这里还有来自加利福尼亚和其他地方的各类水果。一些亲戚和亲爱的老朋友们陪我待了一整天。你认为83年是很长的一段时间，对此我并不奇怪。但对我来说，从我还是一个在黑弗里尔老农场里玩耍、跟你差不多大的小男孩时，到如今似乎也只是短暂的一瞬间。我感谢你美好的祝福，我把同样的祝福送给你。我很高兴你在学校学习，那是一个极好的地方。请代我向沙利文小姐致以最诚挚的问候。我带着深深的爱。

你的老朋友
约翰·G.惠蒂尔

Whittier's Reply

My Dear Young Friend—I was very glad to have such a pleasant letter on my birthday. I had two or three hundred others and thine was one of the most welcome of all. I must tell thee about how the day passed at Oak Knoll. Of course the sun did not shine, but we had great open wood fires in the rooms, which were all very sweet with roses and other flowers, which were sent to me from distant friends; and fruits of all kinds from California and other places. Some relatives and dear old friends were with me through the day. I do not wonder thee thinks eighty-three years a long time, but to me it seems but a very little while since I was a boy no older than thee, playing on the old farm at Haverhill. I thank thee for all thy good wishes, and wish thee as many. I am glad thee is at the Institution; it is an excellent place. Give my best regards to Miss Sullivan, and with a great deal of love I am

Thy old friend.
JOHN G.WIIITTIER.

五

为了小汤米

在下面的几封信中出现的汤米·斯特格,四岁时就失明且失聪。他妈妈去世了,爸爸太穷无法照顾他。有一阵子他被寄放在艾里基尼总医院。从那里又被送到救济院,从那时起,他在宾夕法尼亚州就没有别的地方可去。海伦从匹兹堡的J.G.布朗先生那里听说了这事,布朗先生写信给她,他本来想为汤米请位家庭教师,可没找到。海伦希望汤米来波士顿,当她被告知为汤米请老师要花钱时,她回答说:"我们会筹集到钱的。"于是,她开始请求朋友们捐款,并节省下自己的每一文钱。

亚历山大·格雷汉姆·贝尔先生建议汤米的朋友把他送到波士顿,帕金斯学校的理事同意汤米进入为盲童开办的幼儿园就读。

同时,海伦找到了为汤米募集教育经费的机会。在冬季来临之前,海伦的狗狗"雌狮"被杀害了,于是朋友们募捐想为海伦再买条狗。但海伦却把美国和英国各地人们寄来的捐款捐给了汤米作为教育费用。这笔捐款投入了新用途后,基金增长得很快,可以支付汤米的学费了。4月6日,他进入幼儿园就读。

后来,凯勒小姐写道:"我永远不会忘记:有些钱是一些穷孩子好不容易节省下来的,正是'为了小汤米'这一目标,使那些我从未见过的、近在咫尺或远在天涯的人们，满怀同情之心，迅速地回应了一颗被囚禁的幼小心灵的无声呼喊。"

致乔治·R.科瑞尔先生

（马萨诸塞州南波士顿盲人学校，1891年3月20日）

我亲爱的朋友，科瑞尔先生：——我刚听说，通过韦德先生，您慷慨捐助，想帮我买一条温顺的狗，我非常感谢您的善意。得知自己在别的地方还有亲爱的朋友，我很高兴。这让我觉得所有人都很善良和友爱。我曾经读到过说英国人和美国人是表兄弟姐妹的文章；但我觉得，说我们是兄弟姐妹才更真实。我的朋友们向我描述过您所在的恢宏壮丽的城市，我自己也读过聪慧的英国人写的许多书。我已经读了《伊诺克·阿登》①，还在心中记住了好几个伟大的诗人的诗句。我很渴望穿过海洋，去看望我的英国朋友和他们英明的女王。一次，米斯郡的伯爵来看我，他告诉我女王因为亲切和睿智而深受人民的爱戴。可能有一天，您会吃惊地看到一个陌生的小女孩来到您的办公室；但当您得知这个小女孩喜欢狗和其他动物时，您会哈哈大笑的。我希望您能给她一个吻，就像韦德先生那样。韦德先生又给了我一条狗，他认为这条狗会跟美丽的"雌狮"一样勇敢而忠诚。现在我要告诉您美国的"爱狗人"准备做些什么。他们将寄钱给我，为一位贫穷、聋哑且失明的小孩子捐钱。他的名字叫"汤米"，只有五岁。他的父母很穷，没钱送他去上学；所以，不必给我买狗了，绅士们已决定帮助汤米，以使他的生活像我的一样充满阳光和欢乐。这是不是一个很棒的计划呀？教育能给汤米的心灵带来光明和音乐，然后，他就会感到由衷的快乐。

来自您真诚的小朋友

海伦·A.凯勒

① 《伊诺克·阿登》：是19世纪英国诗人丁尼生所著的叙事诗。

To Mr. George R. Krehl

Institution for the Blind,

(*South Boston, Mass., March 20, 1891.*)

 My Dear Friend, Mr Krehl: —I have just heard, through Mr. Wade, of your kind offer to buy me a gentle dog, and I want to thank you for the kind thought. It makes me very happy indeed to know that I have such dear friends in other lands. It makes me think that all people are good and loving. I have read that the English and Americans are cousins; but I am sure it would be much truer to say that we are brothers and sisters. My friends have told me about your great and magnificent city, and I have read a great deal that wise Englishmen have written. I have begun to read "Enoch Arden," and I know several of the great poet's poems by heart. I am eager to cross the ocean, for I want to see my English friends and their good and wise queen. Once the Earl of Meath came to see me, and he told me that the queen was much beloved by her people, because of her gentleness and wisdom. Some day you will be surprised to see a little strange girl coming into your office; but when you know it is the little girl who loves dogs and all other animals, you will laugh, and I hope you will give her a kiss, just as Mr. Wade does. He has another dog for me, and he thinks she will be as brave and faithful as my beautiful Lioness. And now I want to tell you what the dog lovers in America are going to do. They are going to send me some money for a poor little deaf and dumb and blind child. His name is Tommy, and he is five years old. His parents are too poor to pay to have the little fellow sent to school; so, instead of giving me a dog, the gentlemen are going to help make Tommy's life as bright and joyous as mine. Is it not a beautiful plan? Education will bring light and music into Tommy's soul, and then he cannot help being happy.

 From your loving little friend,
 HELEN A. KELLER.

致奥利弗·温德尔·霍姆斯博士

（马萨诸塞州南波士顿，1891年4月）

亲爱的霍姆斯博士——在这春光明媚的四月天，您对春天的描绘、您那优美的文字，在我心中奏响了音乐。我喜欢《春天》和《春天来了》里的每一个词。我想，当您听到这些诗作教会我去欣赏和热爱美好的春光时，您一定会很高兴的。虽然我看不到宣告春天来临的美丽而纤巧的花朵，也听不见归巢的鸟儿欢快的啁啾，但每当我读到《春天来了》时，哇！我就不再是盲人了，因为我可以用您的眼睛来看，并用您的耳朵来听。当我的诗人在近旁时，慈爱的大自然母亲就没有了秘密。我精心选择了这张信笺纸，因为我想借信角上的那枚紫罗兰花告诉您我的感恩之心。我想让您知道失明且聋哑的小汤米刚刚来到我们可爱的幼儿园。他贫穷无助、孤苦无依，但在四月之后，教育会给汤米的生活带来光明和欢乐。如果您要来的话，您一定会请求波士顿善良的人们也来帮助汤米，点亮他的整个人生。

您真诚的朋友
海伦·A.凯勒

To Dr. Oliver Wendell Holmes

(*South Boston, Mass., April, 1891.*)

Dear Dr. Holmes: —Your beautiful words about spring have been making music in my heart, these bright April days. I love every word of "Spring" and "Spring Has Come." I think you will be glad to hear that these poems have taught me to enjoy and love the beautiful springtime, even though I cannot see the fair, frail blossoms which proclaim its approach, or hear the joyous warbling of the home-coming birds. But when I read "Spring Has Come," lo! I am not blind any longer, for I see with your eyes and hear with your ears. Sweet Mother Nature can have no secrets from me when my poet is near. I have chosen this paper because I want the spray of violets in the corner to tell you of my grateful love. I want you to see baby Tom, the blind and deaf and dumb child who has just come to our pretty garden. He is poor and helpless and lonely now, but before another April education will have brought light and gladness into Tommy's life. If you do come, you will want to ask the kind people of Boston to help brighten Tommy's whole life. Your loving friend,

  HELEN KELLER.

致约翰·埃弗雷特·米莱爵士②

（马萨诸塞州南波士顿帕金斯盲人学校，1891年4月30日）

  我亲爱的米莱先生：您的美国小妹妹之所以给您写信，是因为她想让您知道，当她听说您对我们可怜的"小汤米"非常关心，还寄钱给汤米帮助他接受教育时，她十分高兴。远在英国的人们，能对美国一名无助的小孩表示同情，这是多么感人的事。当我在书中读到对您那宏伟的城市的描述时，我曾想，如果我去访问这个城市，那里的人们对我来说都是陌生人吧。但现在我感觉完全不同了。对我来说，似乎所有人都充满了同情心，大家彼此不再陌生。我迫不及待地想抽时间去看看我亲爱的英国朋友们，还想看看他们美丽的岛国。我最喜爱的诗人曾写下关于英国的几行诗，我非常喜欢这些诗句。我想您也会喜欢它们的，以下是我为您抄录的诗句：

---

②约翰·埃弗雷特·米莱（1829—1896），英国画家与插图画家，也是前拉斐尔派的创始人之一。

握紧巨浪的臂膀，

从海草边缘到山中的石楠，

不列颠的橡树深深扎根，

她柔弱而坚定地立着，

辉映着白色的悬崖和绿色的树荫，

大海紧拥爱抚着她，

在群山和溪流之间，

是我们小巧的母亲岛，愿上帝保佑她！

当您听说有位和蔼的女士在教汤米时，您一定会非常高兴的，汤米现在是个活泼可爱的小家伙了。相比拼写单词，他更喜欢攀爬，也许这是因为目前他还不懂语言是多么奇妙的东西吧。他还想象不出，当他能告诉我们他的想法时，他会多么、多么高兴啊！而我们届时也能告诉他大家一直都很爱他。

明天，四月就要把她的眼泪和羞涩藏到可爱五月的鲜花下面了。我想知道英国的五月天是不是也像我们这里的一样美。

现在我该说再见了。请一直把我看作您亲爱的小妹妹。

海伦·凯勒

To Sir John Everett Millais

(*Perkins Institution for the Blind, South Boston, Mass., April 30, 1891.*)

My Dear Mr. Millais: —Your little American sister is going to write you a letter, because she wants you to know how pleased she was to hear you were interested in our poor little Tommy, and had sent some money to help educate him. It is very beautiful to think that people far away in England feel sorry for a little helpless child in America. I used to think, when I read in my books about your great city, that when I visited it the people would be strangers to me, but now I feel differently. It seems to me that all people who have loving, pitying hearts, are not strangers to each other. I can hardly wait patiently for the time to come when I shall see my dear English friends, and their beautiful island home. My favorite poet has written some lines about England which I love very much. I think you will like them too, so I will try to write them for you.

"Hugged in the clinging billow's clasp,

From seaweed fringe to mountain heather,

The British oak with rooted grasp

Her slender handful holds together,

With cliffs of white and bowers of green,

And ocean narrowing to caress her,

And hills and threaded streams between,

Our little mother isle. God bless her!"

You will be glad to hear that Tommy has a kind lady to teach him, and that he is a pretty, active little fellow. He loves to climb much better than to spell, but that is because he does not know yet what a wonderful thing language is. He cannot imagine how very, very happy he will be when he can tell us his thoughts, and we can tell him how we have loved him so long.

Tomorrow April will hide her tears and blushes beneath the flowers of lovely May. I wonder if the Maydays in England are as beautiful as they are here.

Now I must say good-bye. Please think of me always as your loving little sister,

HELEN KELLER.

致尊敬的菲利普斯·布鲁克斯牧师

（南波士顿，1891年5月1日）

我亲爱的布鲁克斯先生：

在这明媚的五月天，海伦给您带去美好的问候。我的老师刚刚告诉我您已经是一名大主教了，您在各地的朋友们都因为他们所热爱的人被授予了如此之高的荣誉而欢呼雀跃。我不太明白主教的工作是做什么的，但我确信那是很好、很有益的工作。我很高兴我亲爱的朋友——您，睿智勇敢且富有爱心，足以胜任此项工作。每当想到您会对很多人说，即使他们不如上帝所希望的那么和善高尚，上帝仍然仁慈地热爱万物，我就感到这一切非常美好。我希望你能告诉人们好消息，他们会高兴得心跳加快的。我也希望，布鲁克斯主教的整个人生能充满快乐，宛如五月充满了鲜花和欢唱的小鸟。

来自您真诚的小朋友

海伦·凯勒

To Rev. Phillips Brooks

(*So. Boston, May 1, 1891.*)

My Dear Mr. Brooks:

Helen sends you a loving greeting this bright Mayday. My teacher has just told me that you have been made a bishop, and that your friends everywhere are rejoicing because one whom they love has been greatly honored. I do not understand very well what a bishop's work is, but I am sure it must be good and helpful, and I am glad that my dear friend is brave, and wise, and loving enough to do it. It is very beautiful to think that you can tell so many people of the heavenly Father's tender love for all His children even when they are not gentle and noble as He wishes them to be. I hope the glad news which you will tell them will make their hearts beat fast with joy and love. I hope too, that Bishop

Brooks' whole life will be as rich in happiness as the month of May is full of blossoms and singing birds.

From your loving little friend,
HELEN KELLER.

在为汤米找到老师之前，他是由海伦和沙利文小姐照顾的，幼儿园为汤米开了欢迎会。在海伦的请求下，布鲁克斯主教在会上发表了致辞。海伦写给报社的信，收到了许多回信。她亲自一一作答，还在报纸上公开发表了感谢信。在这封写给《波士顿先驱报》编辑的信中，附有完整的捐助者名单。捐款合计超过1600美元。

致约翰·H.霍姆斯先生

（南波士顿，1891年5月13日）

《波士顿先驱报》的编辑：

亲爱的霍姆斯先生——您能在贵报上刊登信后所附的名册吗？我认为贵报的读者会高兴地知道有这么多人为小汤米所做的事，他们也希望分享帮助他的快乐。汤米在幼儿园过得十分愉快，每天都能学到新东西。他已经发现了门有锁，小棍和纸条能很容易地插进锁眼里；但当他把这些东西放进去后，却又不急于把它们拿出来。比起拼写，他更喜欢爬床柱和扭开蒸汽阀门，这是因为他还不懂词汇能帮助他发现更多崭新而有趣的事物。我希望好心人能继续为汤米捐助，直到为汤米筹集到充足的教育经费。教育已给他的生活带来了光明和音乐。

您的小朋友
海伦·凯勒

To Mr. John H. Holmes

(*South Boston, May 13, 1891.*)

Editor of the *Boston Herald*:

My Dear Mr. Holmes: —Will you kindly print in the *Herald*, the enclosed list? I think the readers of your paper will be glad to know that so much has been done for dear little Tommy, and that they will all wish to share in the pleasure of helping him. He is very happy indeed at the kindergarten, and is learning something every day. He has found out that doors have locks, and that little sticks and bits of paper can be got into the keyhole quite easily; but he does not seem very eager to get them out after they are in. He loves to climb the bed-posts and unscrew the steam valves much better than to spell, but that is because he does not understand that words would help him to make new and interesting discoveries. I hope that good people will continue to work for Tommy until his fund is completed, and education has brought light and music into his little life. From your little friend,

HELEN KELLER.

致奥利弗·温德尔·霍姆斯博士

（南波士顿，1891年5月27日）

亲爱的、温文尔雅的诗人——如果海伦老写信打扰您，我害怕您会把她想成一个令人讨厌的小姑娘。但是，当您为了使她快乐而做了许多事之后，她应该如何才能向您传递爱和感激的信息呢？我忍不住想告诉您，当阿纳戈诺斯先生把您要给"小汤米"钱，帮助他受教育的事告诉我后，我是多么高兴啊！我知道您没有忘记那可爱的孩子，因为您带来的礼物满载着温柔的同情心，我很遗憾地告诉您汤米还没有学会任何单

词。他仍是您曾看到过的那个好动的小家伙。可是转念一想，他能在明亮的新家里快乐地嬉戏，这也是件令人愉快的事。渐渐地，那被老师称作"思想"的奇特而美妙的东西，将开始张开美丽的翅膀，飞舞着找寻知识的土壤。而语言就是"思想"的翅膀，对吗？

自从跟您见面之后，我就去了安多弗，我对朋友们告诉我的关于菲利普斯学院的事很感兴趣，因为我知道您曾在过那里，我感觉得到那个地方对您是多么亲切。我努力去想象我那彬彬有礼的诗人，当他还是个小男生时是什么样子的。我想知道他是不是在安多弗了解了鸟儿的歌声，并懂得了羞涩林中孩童的秘密？我相信他的心中充满了音乐，在上帝的美丽世界里，他听到了爱的甜美回音。当我回家时，老师给我读了《男生》这首诗，因为这首诗还没有印成盲文。

您知道下星期二下午，盲童将在翠蒙堂举行毕业典礼吗？我给您在信里放了张票，希望您能来。我们会自豪而高兴地欢迎我们的诗人朋友的到来。我将朗诵赞美阳光灿烂的意大利美丽城市的作品。我希望我们善良的朋友爱利斯博士也能来，并抱一抱汤米。

送上我深深的爱和一个吻。来自您的小朋友。

海伦·A. 凯勒

To Dr. Oliver Wendell Holmes

(*South Boston, May 27, 1891.*)

Dear, Gentle Poet: —I fear that you will think Helen a very troublesome little girl if she writes to you too often; but how is she to help sending you loving and grateful messages, when you do so much to make her glad? I cannot begin to tell you how delighted I was when Mr. Anagnos told me that you had sent him some money to help educate "Baby Tom." Then I knew that you had not forgotten the dear little child, for the gift brought with it the thought of tender sympathy. I am very sorry to say that Tommy has not learned any words yet. He is the same restless little creature he was when you saw him. But it is pleasant to think that he is happy and playful in his bright new home, and by and by that strange, wonderful thing teacher calls *mind*, will begin to spread its beautiful wings and fly away in search of knowledge-land. Words are the mind's wings, are they not?

 I have been to Andover since I saw you, and I was greatly interested in all that my friends told me about Phillips Academy, because I knew you had been there, and I felt it was a place dear to you. I tried to imagine my gentle poet when he was a school-boy, and I wondered if it was in Andover he learned the songs of the birds and the secrets of the shy little woodland children. I am sure his heart was always full of music and in God's beautiful world he must have heard love's sweet replying. When I came home teacher read to me "The School-boy," for it is not in our print.

 Did you know that the blind children are going to have their commencement exercises in Tremont Temple, next Tuesday afternoon? I enclose a ticket, hoping that you will come. We shall all be proud and happy to welcome our poet friend. I shall recite about the beautiful cities of sunny Italy. I hope our kind friend Dr. Ellis will come too, and take Tom in his arms.

 With much love and a kiss, from your little friend,
 HELEN A. KELLER.

致尊敬的菲利普斯·布鲁克斯

（南波士顿，1891年6月8日）

亲爱的布鲁克斯先生：

我遵照承诺把照片寄给您，并且希望在这个夏天，当您看到这张照片时，您的思绪会飞到南方您快乐的小朋友身旁。我曾经希望我能像用手欣赏雕塑一样"看到"照片，但现在我不这样想了，因为我亲爱的父亲已让我脑子里装满了美丽的画面，甚至有我看不到的东西。亲爱的布鲁克斯先生，如果您的眼睛里也没有光亮，那么您就能更好地体会，当小海伦听着老师给她解释世界上那些她既看不到又摸不着，只能用心去感受的最好、最美的东西时，她心里是多么高兴啊。每一天，我都能发现一些令我快乐的事。昨天，我第一次觉得"做运动"是件很美妙的事，似乎万物都在努力靠近上帝，您也是这样认为的吗？现在是星期天早上，我坐在图书馆里写这封信，而您正在教导成百上千的人们有关天父的伟大和仁爱的事迹。您是不是非常快乐？当您成为一位主教后，您将向更多的人布道，从而让更多的人更加快乐。老师向您转达诚挚的问候，我也随同照片送上我的真诚的爱。

来自您的小朋友

海伦·凯勒

To Rev. Phillips Brooks

(*South Boston, June 8, 1891.*)

My dear Mr. Brooks,

I send you my picture as I promised, and I hope when you look at it this summer your thoughts will fly southward to your happy little friend. I used to wish that I could see pictures with my hands as I do statues, but now I do not often think about it because my dear Father has filled my mind with beautiful pictures, even of things I cannot see. If the light were not in your eyes, dear Mr.

Brooks, you would understand better how happy your little Helen was when her teacher explained to her that the best and most beautiful things in the world cannot be seen nor even touched, but just felt in the heart. Every day I find out something which makes me glad. Yesterday I thought for the first time what a beautiful thing motion was, and it seemed to me that everything was trying to get near to God, does it seem that way to you? It is Sunday morning, and while I sit here in the library writing this letter you are teaching hundreds of people some of the grand and beautiful things about their heavenly Father. Are you not very, very happy? and when you are a Bishop you will preach to more people and more and more will be made glad. Teacher sends her kind remembrances, and I send you with my picture my dear love.

 From your little friend
 HELEN KELLER.

六

发表的文章

6月，帕金斯学校放假，海伦和她的老师南下回到塔斯坎比亚，她们在那一直待到12月。这几个月的通信中断了，起因是《霜之王》抄袭事件对海伦和沙利文小姐产生了不良影响，令她们灰心丧气。当时，这似乎是个大麻烦，给她们带来了很多不快。在其他文章里有关于这一事件的分析，海伦对此也做了解释。

致阿尔伯特·H.蒙塞尔先生[①]

（布鲁斯特，1892年3月10日）

亲爱的蒙塞尔先生：

其实不需要我告诉您，您的信是多么受欢迎。我欣赏您信中的每一个词，并希望信能再长点。当我读到您描述老海神尼普顿[②]的喜怒无常时，我哈哈大笑。自从我们到布鲁斯特后，他确实行为古怪。显然有什么事触犯了这位陛下，但我想不出是什么事。他的表达方式也很混乱，以至

[①] 阿尔伯特·H.蒙塞尔（1858—1918），美国教育家、色彩学家和美术家，1898年创立以色彩的三要素为基础的色彩表示法。

[②] 尼普顿：罗马神话中的海神，他在罗马也被作为马神崇拜，管理赛马活动。

于我不敢把您的友好信息转告他。天知道这是怎么了！也许是当"老海神"睡在海边时，听到了万物生长的轻柔乐曲——那是在大地胸怀里生命的悸动，于是他那狂暴的心无比愤怒，因为他知道自己和冬天的统治即将结束。绝望的暴君们联合起来要做最后一搏，他们认为，当温和的春天看到被他们的暴力摧残过的万物时，一定会落荒而逃的。可是，哦！可爱的春姑娘只是笑得更甜，朝着敌人筑造的冰城堡吹了口气，一瞬间，它们就土崩瓦解了。欢乐的大地用皇家仪式来欢迎春姑娘。但是，当我再次见到您时，我必须抛弃这些想入非非的幻想。请代我向您的母亲问好。老师想说她很喜欢那些照片，我们回来以后，她想看看能不能拿几张。现在，亲爱的朋友，请接受这些问候，因为这里面饱含着爱。

您真诚的
海伦·凯勒

To Mr. Albert H. Munsell

(*Brewster, Mar. 10, 1892.*)

My dear Mr. Munsell,

Surely I need not tell you that your letter was very welcome. I enjoyed every word of it and wished that it was longer. I laughed when you spoke of old Neptune's wild moods. He has, in truth, behaved very strangely ever since we came to Brewster. It is evident that something has displeased his Majesty but I cannot imagine what it can be. His expression has been so turbulent that I have feared to give him your kind message. Who knows! Perhaps the Old Sea God as he lay asleep upon the shore, heard the soft music of growing things—the stir of life in the earth's bosom, and his stormy heart was angry, because he knew that his and Winter's reign was almost at an end. So together the unhappy monarch[s] fought most despairingly, thinking that gentle Spring would turn and fly at the very sight of the havoc caused by their forces. But lo! the lovely maiden only smiles more sweetly, and breathes upon the icy battlements of her enemies, and in a moment they vanish, and the glad Earth gives her a royal welcome. But I must put away these idle fancies until we meet again. Please give your dear mother my love. Teacher wishes me to say that she liked the photograph very much and she will see about having some when we return. Now, dear friend, please accept these few words because of the love that is linked with them.

Lovingly yours
HELEN KELLER.

下面这封写给《圣·尼古拉斯》编辑们的信，信中没有日期，但应该是写于被公开发表之前的两三个月内。

致《圣·尼古拉斯》编辑的信

尊敬的《圣·尼古拉斯》编辑：

我很高兴给你们寄去我的亲笔信，因为我希望那些阅读《圣·尼古拉斯》的孩子们能知道盲童是怎样书写的。我想他们当中有些人肯定想知道我们是如何让线条保持笔直的，所以我会告诉他们是怎么做到这点的。我们都有一块带凹槽的书写板，在写字的时候，我们就把书写板夹在要书写的页面中间；平行的凹槽就相当于横线，再用钝铅笔在纸上书写，就很容易让单词保持齐平。小型字母都可以写在槽里，但过长的字母则会上下超出槽外。我们用右手握铅笔，用左手的食指仔细感知字母的构成和空格。刚开始很难保持水平，但如果我们坚持不懈地尝试，慢慢就容易了。经过大量的练习，我们就可以字迹清晰地写信给我们的朋友们。这时，我们会非常非常高兴的。有时人们会访问盲人学校，如果他们来的话，我相信他们一定希望看看学生们是怎样书写的。

您十分真诚的小朋友

海伦·凯勒

To *St. Nicholas*

Dear St. Nicholas:

It gives me very great pleasure to send you my autograph because I want the boys and girls who read *St. Nicholas* to know how blind children write. I suppose some of them wonder how we keep the lines so straight so I will try to tell them how it is done. We have a grooved board which we put between the pages when we wish to write. The parallel grooves correspond to lines and when we have pressed the paper into them by means of the blunt end of the pencil it is very easy to keep the words even. The small letters are all made in the grooves, while the long ones extend above and below them. We guide the pencil with the right hand, and feel carefully with the forefinger of the left hand to see that we shape and space the letters correctly. It is very difficult at first to form them plainly, but if we keep on trying it gradually becomes easier, and after a great deal of practice we can write legible letters to our friends. Then we are very, very happy. Sometime they may visit a school for the blind. If they do, I am sure they will wish to see the pupils write.

Very sincerely your little friend

HELEN KELLER.

1892年5月，海伦为帕金斯盲童幼儿园举办了一次茶会。这基本上是她自己的主意，房子由玛伦·D.斯波尔丁女士，也就是约翰·P.斯波尔丁的

姐姐提供。她是海伦最好的、最慷慨的朋友之一。茶会为盲童们筹集了超过2000美元的捐款。

致卡罗琳·德比小姐

（南波士顿，1892年5月9日）

我亲爱的卡莉小姐——我很高兴收到您的来信。难道还要我告诉您，得知您对"茶会"感兴趣，我是多么高兴吗？当然我们一定不能放弃这次活动。很快我就要远行，回到我温暖的家中。在阳光灿烂的南方，每当我想到亲爱的波士顿的朋友们为了使盲童幸福而做的事，我就无比高兴。他们使许多几乎看不见的孩子生活得更幸福和更快乐。我知道那些善良的人们总是不由自主地对那些看不见明亮光线，也看不见能为其带来欢乐的奇妙事物的小孩子们抱有同情心。在我看来，所有的同情心都应以仁慈的行动来表现；当那些无助的小盲童知道我们在为他们的幸福而努力时，他们也会来参加"茶会"，让它取得成功的。并且我相信，我将成为世界上最快乐的小姑娘。请让布鲁克斯主教知悉我们的计划，这样，他就会安排时间来参加我们的活动。我很高兴埃莉诺小姐对这件事也很感兴趣。请代我向她问好。我明天去看您，并做好下一步的计划。请代我和老师向您亲爱的阿姨问好，告诉她我们很喜欢这次短暂旅行。

爱您的
海伦·凯勒

To Miss Caroline Derby

(*South Boston*, May 9, 1892.)

My dear Miss Carrie: —I was much pleased to receive your kind letter. Need I tell yon that I was more than delighted to hear that you are really interested in the"tea"? Of course we must not give it up. Very soon I am going far away, to my own dear home, in the sunny south, and it would always make me happy to think that the last thing which my dear friends in Boston did for my pleasure was to help make the lives of many little sightless children good and happy. I know that kind people cannot help feeling a tender sympathy for the little ones, who cannot see the beautiful light, or any of the wonderful things which give them pleasure; and it seems to me that all loving sympathy must express itself in acts of kindness; and when the friends of little helpless blind children understand that we are working for their happiness, they will come and make our "tea" a success, and I am sure I shall be the happiest little girl in all the world. Please let Bishop Brooks know our plans, so that he may arrange to be with us. I am glad Miss Eleanor is interested. Please give her my love. I will see you tomorrow and then we can make the rest of our plans. Please give your dear aunt teacher's and my love and tell her that we enjoyed our little visit very much indeed.

Lovingly yours,

HELEN KELLER.

致爱德华·H.克莱门特先生

（南波士顿，1892年5月18日）

亲爱的克莱门特先生——我在这样一个美丽的早晨给您写信，是因为我心里盈满了欢乐，想让您和在"副刊"办公室的我亲爱的朋友们也一起高兴一下。茶会的准备工作快完成了，我满心期待着这次活动。我知道我不能失败。当善良的人们知道我在为无助的、生活在黑暗和无知中的孩子们寻求帮助时，他们是不会让我失望的。他们会来参加茶会，并购买"光明"——美丽的知识之光和对无依无靠的盲童的爱。我还清

楚地记得我亲爱的老师来到我身边时的情景。当时的我心中没有光明，就像那些小盲童一样，正等着进幼儿园。那个充满阳光和美景的神奇世界在我面前被隐藏起来了，我做梦都没想到它会如此美妙。终于，老师来了，教会我用小小的手指去握住那些美丽的钥匙，黑暗的牢笼之门被开启，我的心灵自由了。

  我真心希望和其他人分享我的快乐，我请求波士顿善良的人们帮助我，给那些小盲童们带去光明和幸福。

爱您的小朋友
海伦·凯勒

To Mr. Edward H · Clement

(*South Boston, May 18th, 1892.*)

  Mr. dear Mr. Clement: —I am going to write to you this beautiful morning because my heart is brimful of happiness and I want you and all my dear friends in the *Transcript* office to rejoice with me. The preparations for my tea are nearly completed, and I am looking forward joyfully to the event. I know I shall not fail. Kind people will not disappoint me, when they know that I plead for helpless little children who live in darkness and ignorance. They will come to my tea and buy light, —the beautiful light of knowledge and love for many little ones who are blind and friendless. I remember perfectly when my dear teacher came to me. Then I was like the little blind children who are waiting to enter the kindergarten. There was no light in my soul. This wonderful world with all its sunlight and beauty was hidden from me, and I had never dreamed of its loveliness. But teacher came to me and taught my little fingers to use the beautiful key that has unlocked the door of my dark prison and set my spirit free.

  It is my earnest wish to share my happiness with others, and I ask the kind people of Boston to help me make the lives of little blind children brighter and happier.

　　Lovingly your little friend,
　　HELEN HELLER.

　　12岁的海伦·凯勒的写作能力开始得到广泛的认可，她已经开始从事系统性写作。

致约翰·希茨先生

（亚拉巴马州塔斯坎比亚，1892年12月19日）

我亲爱的希茨先生：

　　我真不知道该如何提笔写这封信。我收到您的信已经很长时间了，如果我要给您回信的话，我有许许多多的话要写。您一定想知道我为什么没有及时给您回信吧，也许您会认为老师和我都很顽皮。如果真是这样的话，那么当我告诉您一些事时，您会很难过的。老师的眼睛一直很痛，导致她不能给任何人写信；而我也在努力完成上个夏天许下的诺言。在我离开波士顿之前，我答应《青年之友》撰写反映我生活的系列文章，我打算在假期里来写；但我身体不太好，以至于我甚至无法给我的朋友写信。当秋高气爽的时节来临时，我感觉自己强健了一些，于是才开始考虑约稿的事了。我花了些时间来制定适合自己的计划。您看，动笔写自己的故事也不是一件太令人愉快的事。尽管如此，最终，我还是根据老师的要求，一点一点地开始了。我着手把零碎的东西拼凑在一起，这并不是件容易的任务，虽然我每天都在做，但我直到一星期前的周六才完成。刚一写完，我就赶快把稿子寄给《青年之友》；但我还不知道他们会不会采用。从那时起，我的身体又不太好，于是我不得不静静休养；

可今天我又好一些了，我希望明天自己的身体能更好。

您在报纸上读到的关于我的报道是不真实的。我们收到您寄来的《沉默的工人报》之后，我立即写信给编辑告诉他弄错了。尽管有时我身体不太好，但我不是个"残废"，我的情况也算不上"悲惨"。

我多么喜欢您的来信啊！每当在收到的信中，蕴含着睿智的思想，我就无比高兴，并想把这些字句永远珍藏在我的记忆中。正如罗斯金先生所说，我的那些书籍里充满了财富，所以我深深地珍爱它们。直到我开始为《青年之友》写稿时，我才意识到书籍是多么宝贵的财富，它们赐予了我的生活多少幸福啊！我现在比任何时候都幸福，因为我意识到幸福正向我走来。我希望您能经常给我写信。每次收到您的来信，老师和我都非常高兴。我想写信给贝尔先生，并寄去我的照片。因为我猜想他很忙，没时间写信给他的小朋友。我时常想起上个春天我们在波士顿一起度过的美好时光。

现在我要告诉您个秘密。我想我们，包括老师、我父亲、小妹妹和我自己，明年三月，将游览华盛顿！！！届时，我又能见到您、亲爱的贝尔先生、埃尔希和戴西了！如果还能见到普拉特夫人，那是不是一件令人非常愉快的事？我想写信给她，也告诉她这个秘密……

您真诚的小朋友
海伦·凯勒

附言：老师说您想知道我希望拥有什么宠物。其实我喜欢所有活泼的生物——我想所有人都是这样的；当然我不能拥有一座小动物园。我已经有了一匹漂亮的小马驹和一只大狗。我还想要只小狗抱在腿上，或者一只大猫咪（在塔斯坎比亚没有好猫）和一只鹦鹉。我想感受一下鹦鹉学舌，那一定很有趣！但是，无论您送我什么样的小动物，我都会很高兴地宠爱它的。

H.K.

To Mr. John Hitz

(*Tuscumbia, Alabama, Dec. 19, 1892.*)

My Dear Mr. Hitz,

I hardly know how to begin a letter to you, it has been such a long time since your kind letter reached me, and there is so much that I would like to write if I could. You must have wondered why your letter has not had an answer, and perhaps you have thought Teacher and me very naughty indeed. If so, you will be very sorry when I tell you something. Teacher's eyes have been hurting her so that she could not write to any one, and I have been trying to fulfil a promise which I made last summer. Before I left Boston, I was asked to write a sketch of my life for the *Youth's Companion*. I had intended to write the sketch during my vacation: but I was not well, and I did not feel able to write even to my friends. But when the bright, pleasant autumn days came, and I felt strong again I began to think about the sketch. It was some time before I could plan it to suit me. You see, it is not very pleasant to write all about one's self. At last, however, I got something bit by bit that Teacher thought would do, and I set about putting the scraps together, which was not an easy task: for, although I worked some on it every day, I did not finish it until a week ago Saturday. I sent the sketch to the *Companion* as soon as it was finished; but I do not know that they will accept it. Since then, I have not been well, and I have been obliged to keep very quiet, and rest; but to-day I am better, and tomorrow I shall be well again, I hope.

The reports which you have read in the paper about me are not true at all. We received the *Silent Worker* which you sent, and I wrote right away to the editor to tell him that it was a mistake. Sometimes I am not well; but I am not a "wreck," and there is nothing "distressing" about my condition.

I enjoyed your dear letter so much! I am always delighted when anyone writes me a beautiful thought which I can treasure in my memory forever. It is because my books are full of the riches of which Mr. Ruskin speaks that I love them so dearly. I did not realize until I began to write the sketch for the *Companion*, what precious companions books have been to me, and how blessed even my life has been: and now I am happier than ever because I do realize the happiness that has come to me. I hope you will write to me as often as you can. Teacher and I are always delighted to hear from you. I want to write to Mr. Bell and send him my picture. I suppose he has been too busy to write to his little friend. I often think of the pleasant time we had all, together in Boston last spring.

Now I am going to tell you a secret. I think we, Teacher, and my father and little sister, and myself, will visit Washington next March!!! Then I shall see you, and dear Mr. Bell, and Elsie and Daisy again! Would not it be lovely if Mrs. Pratt could meet us there? I think I will write to her and tell her the secret too...

Lovingly your little friend,

HELEN KELLER.

P. S. Teacher says you want to know what kind of a pet I would like to have. I love all living things, —I suppose everyone does; but of course I cannot have a menagerie. I have a beautiful pony, and a large dog. And I would like a little dog to hold in my lap, or a big pussy (there are no fine cats in Tuscumbia) or a parrot. I would like to feel a parrot talk, it would be so much fun! but I would be pleased with, and love any little creature you send me.

H. K.

3月，海伦和沙利文小姐前往北方，随后的几个月她们一边旅行一边拜访朋友。

阅读这封描述尼亚加拉大瀑布的信时，我们应知道海伦是了解距离和形状的，当她通过实地探索，穿过大桥，乘电梯下行后，她对尼亚加拉大瀑布的规模也有了印象。特别重要的细节是：她通过把手放在玻璃窗上感觉到水流的冲击。贝尔博士给了她一个鸭绒垫子，她把垫子紧贴身上，以增强对震动的感受。

致凯特·亚当斯·凯勒夫人

（南波士顿，4月13日）

……真想不到，老师、普拉特夫人和我决定与亲爱的贝尔博士一起去旅行。

威斯特维尔特先生是父亲在华盛顿认识的一位绅士，他在罗切斯特市有一所聋哑学校。我们先去那里……

一天下午，威斯特维尔特先生为我们举行了一场招待会，来了很多人。有些人问了我很奇怪的问题。有位女士似乎对我喜欢花感到很吃惊，因为我看不到花的美丽颜色。当我坚定地告诉她我喜欢花时，她说："毫无疑问您是用手指来感受花的颜色的。"当然，我们喜欢花绝不只是因为它们鲜艳的颜色……有位绅士问我怎样看待"美"。我承认一开始我被问得有点不知所措，但一分钟后我回答说，"美"就是"善良"的一种形式，于是那位绅士走开了。

招待会结束后，我们回到酒店，老师睡着了，对为她准备的惊喜一无所知。这个惊喜是我和贝尔先生一起计划的，在我们告诉老师之前，贝尔先生先安排好了一切。这个惊喜就是——我将很高兴地跟我亲爱的老师一起去看尼亚加拉大瀑布！……

酒店离河很近，我把手放在窗子上就能感觉到水流的冲击。第二天一早，温暖而明亮的太阳升起后，我们迅速起床，心里满是欢快的期待……您永远也想象不出当我站在尼亚加拉大瀑布旁时的感受，除非您也能亲身体验一下这种神奇的感受。我几乎意识不到脚下的急流正愤怒

地奔驰、跳跃和咆哮。这急流如同某个有生命的事物正在奔向那可怕的命运一样。我希望自己能描述出大瀑布的原貌、它的美丽和极致的壮观，以及水流从悬崖峭壁的山脊上奔流而下的无穷魅力。在这种宏大的力量面前，人会感到无助和不知所措。当我第一次站在大海边，感受着惊涛拍岸时，也同样有这种感觉。在寂静的夜晚，当您凝望着星星时，我猜想您也会有这种感觉，我说的对不对呢？……我们乘电梯下行了120英尺，以观赏瀑布下幽深峡谷里湍急的漩涡和涡流。距离瀑布2英里的地方有一座宏伟的悬索桥。它横跨峡谷，高出水面258英尺，两端由坚固的岩石砌成的塔楼支撑，两塔相距800英尺。当我们来到加拿大这边时，我大叫："天佑女王！"（《天佑女王》是英国皇室和加拿大皇室的颂歌。）可是老师却说我是个小"叛徒"。但我可不这样想，我不过是身在加拿大，入乡随俗罢了。此外，我也很尊重英明的英国女王。

  亲爱的妈妈，当您听到有一位名叫胡珂的善良小姐正在努力帮我提高说话水平时，您一定会高兴的。哦，我多么希望并虔诚祈祷有一天我也能侃侃而谈啊！……

  上星期天晚上，蒙塞尔先生和我们在一起。如果您也能听他讲讲威尼斯的见闻，那么您肯定会很高兴的！他生动逼真的口头描述使我们感觉自己仿佛正坐在圣马可广场的阴凉处幻想着，或航行在月色朦胧的运河上……我希望有一天当我游览威尼斯时，蒙塞尔先生能和我同行。这简直是一个想入非非的白日梦啦。您要知道，在我所有的朋友中，只有他能描绘得如此精彩、如此美妙……

To Mrs. Kate Adams Keller

(*South Boston, April 13.*)

…Teacher, Mrs. Pratt and I very unexpectedly decided to take a journey with dear Dr Bell

Mr. Westervelt, a gentleman whom father met in Washington, has a school for the deaf in Rochester. We went there first…

Mr. Westervelt gave us a reception one afternoon. A great many people came. Some of them asked odd questions. A lady seemed surprised that I loved flowers when I could not see their beautiful colors, and when I assured her I did love them, she said, "no doubt you feel the colors with your fingers." But of course, it is not alone for their bright colors that we love the flowers … A gentleman asked me what *beauty* meant to my mind. I must confess I was puzzled at first. But after a minute I answered that beauty was a form of goodness—and he went away.

When the reception was over we went back to the hotel and teacher slept quite unconscious of the surprise which was in store for her. Mr. Bell and I planned it together, and Mr. Bell made all the arrangements before we told teacher anything about it. This was the surprise—I was to have the pleasure of taking my dear teacher to see Niagara Falls!…

The hotel was so near the river that I could feel it rushing past by putting my hand on the window. The next morning the sun rose bright and warm, and we got up quickly for our hearts were full of pleasant expectation… You can never imagine how I felt when I stood in the presence of Niagara until you have the same mysterious sensations yourself. I could hardly realize that it was water that I felt rushing and plunging with impetuous fury at my feet. It seemed as if it were some living thing rushing on to some terrible fate. I wish I could describe the cataract as it is, its beauty and awful grandeur, and the fearful and irresistible plunge of its waters over the brow of the precipice. One feels helpless and overwhelmed in the presence of such a vast force. I had the same feeling once before when I first stood by the great ocean and felt its waves beating against the shore. I suppose you feel so, too, when you gaze up to the stars in the stillness of the night, do you not?…We went down a hundred and twenty feet in an elevator that we might see the violent eddies and whirlpools in the deep gorge below the Falls. Within two miles of the Falls is a wonderful suspension bridge. It is thrown across the gorge at a height of two hundred and fifty-eight feet above the water and is supported on each bank by towers of solid rock, which are eight hundred feet apart. When we crossed over to the Canadian side, I cried, "God save the Queen!" Teacher said I was a little traitor. But I do not think so. I was only doing as the Canadians do, while I was in their country, and besides I honor England's good queen.

You will be pleased, dear Mother, to hear that a kind lady whose name is Miss Hooker is endeavoring to improve my speech. Oh, I do so hope and pray that I shall speak well some day!…

Mr. Munsell spent last Sunday evening with us. How you would have enjoyed hearing him tell about Venice! His beautiful word-pictures made us feel as if [we] were sitting in the shadow of San Marco, dreaming, or sailing upon the moonlit canal…I hope when I visit Venice, as I surely shall some day, that Mr. Munsell will go with me. That is my castle in the air. You see, none of my friends describe things to me so vividly and so beautifully as he does…

海伦在写给约翰·P. 斯波尔丁先生的一封信里描述了她参观世界博览会的见闻，这封信被刊登在《圣·尼古拉斯》杂志上，信的内容基本与致卡罗琳·德比小姐的书信一致。在沙利文小姐为杂志刊文所写的导读语中，提到人们常常会对她说："海伦用手指看到的东西比我们用眼睛看到的东西还多得多。"

致负责建筑群和展览的相关部门的主管和职员

先生们——此信件持有人为海伦·凯勒小姐，她由沙利文小姐陪同，希望能全面参观博览会的各个展区。她是一位盲聋人，但她能同别人交流。据介绍，她有一种奇妙的能力，可以了解她所参观过的事物，她还具有超越其年龄的高位智力和文化水平。请各位为她参观展区的展品提供便利条件，并尽可能对她给予特殊优待。

感谢各位的支持。

您真诚的

（签名）博览会会长 H.N. 希金博特姆

To the Chiefs of the Departments and Officers in Charge of Buildings and Exhibits

Gentlemen—The bearer, Miss Helen Keller, accompanied by Miss Sullivan, is desirous of making a complete inspection of the Exposition in all Departments. She is blind and deaf, but is able to converse, and is introduced to me as one having a wonderful ability to understand the objects she visits, and as being possessed of a high order of intelligence and of culture beyond her years. Please favor her with every facility to examine the exhibits in the several Departments, and extend to her such other courtesies as may be possible.

Thanking you in advance for the same, I am, with respect,

Very truly yours,

(signed) H. N. HIGINBOTHAM, PRESIDENT.

致卡罗琳·德比小姐

（宾夕法尼亚州希尔顿，1893 年 8 月 17 日）

……博览会上的每个人都对我很友好……几乎所有的参展商都非常愿意让我触摸那些精美绝伦的展品，他们还耐心地向我讲解每一样展品。一位我已记不得名字的法国绅士，向我展示了精湛的法国青铜器。我觉

得这些青铜器是博览会上给我带来最多快乐的展品；它们栩栩如生，摸起来让人感觉很奇妙。贝尔博士陪同我们参观了电子大厦，向我们展示了一些颇具历史意义的电话。我看到了一部电话，在那次世纪博览会上，巴西皇帝佩德罗二世曾通过它听到了从远处传来的"生存还是死亡"的经典台词。伊利诺伊州的吉勒特博士带我们参观了文艺大厦和妇女大厦。在文艺大厦，我们参观了蒂芙尼展厅，试握了华光璀璨、价值10万美元的蒂芙尼钻石，还触摸了其他许多稀有而价值不菲的珍宝。我坐在路德维希国王的扶手椅上，当吉勒特博士评价说我有许多忠实的臣民时，我感觉自己就像个女王。在妇女大厦，我们遇到了俄国的玛利亚·斯考威斯克公主，还有一位漂亮的叙利亚女郎，我很喜欢她俩。此外，我还和著名演讲家莫斯教授去了日本馆。当我看到那些妙趣横生的展品后，才知道日本人充满了奇思妙想。从他们制造的大量玩具可以判断，日本是孩子的天堂。那些造型奇特的日本乐器和漂亮的工艺品都很引人注目。日本的书籍也别具一格。在它们的字符表上有47个音图（假名）。莫斯教授睿智而亲切，他对日本很了解。他邀请我下次到波士顿时去参观他在塞伦的博物馆。总之，我最喜欢的还是在平静的泻湖上泛舟，朋友们向我描述了绮丽的风景，我认为这是博览会最壮观的一幕。我们曾在水面上飘荡，夕阳西下，白城建筑群笼罩在玫瑰色的柔光中，看上去宛如一个梦幻世界……

当然，我们还游览了"大道乐园"。那是个令人眼花缭乱、心醉神迷的地方。我骑着骆驼在开罗的街道上行进，真是太好玩啦！我们还坐了摩天轮和冰道火车，又坐着鲸背船航行……

To Miss Caroline Derby

Hulton, Penn., August 17, 1893.

…Every one at the Fair was very kind to me…Nearly all of the exhibitors seemed perfectly willing to let me touch the most delicate things, and they were very nice about explaining everything to me. A French gentleman, whose name I cannot remember, showed me the great French bronzes. I believe they gave me more pleasure than anything else at the Fair: they were so lifelike and wonderful to my touch. Dr. Bell went with us himself to the electrical building, and showed us some of the historical telephones. I saw the one through which Emperor Dom Pedro listened to the words, "To be, or not to be," at the Centennial. Dr. Gillett of Illinois took us to the Liberal Arts and Woman's buildings. In the former I visited Tiffany's exhibit, and held the beautiful Tiffany diamond, which is valued at one hundred thousand dollars, and touched many other rare and costly things. I sat in King Ludwig's armchair and felt like a queen when Dr. Gillett remarked that I had many loyal subjects. At the Woman's building we met the Princess Maria Schaovskoy of Russia, and a beautiful Syrian lady. I liked them both very much. I went to the Japanese department with Prof. Morse who is a well-known lecturer. I never realized what a wonderful people the Japanese are until I saw their most interesting exhibit. Japan must indeed be a paradise for children to judge from the great number of playthings which are manufactured there. The queer-looking Japanese musical instruments, and their beautiful works of art were interesting. The Japanese books are very odd. There are forty-seven letters in their alphabets. Prof. Morse knows a great deal about Japan, and is very kind and wise. He invited me to visit his museum in Salem the next time I go to Boston. But I think I enjoyed the sails on the tranquil lagoon, and the lovely scenes, as my friends described them to me, more than anything else at the Fair. Once, while we were out on the water, the sun went down over the rim of the earth, and threw a soft, rosy light over the White City, making it look more than ever like Dreamland…

 Of course, we visited the Midway Plaisance. It was a bewildering and fascinating place. I went into the streets of Cairo, and rode on the camel. That was fine fun. We also rode in the Ferris wheel, and on the ice-railway, and had a sail in the Whaleback…

　　1893年春，塔斯坎比亚成立了一个俱乐部，凯勒夫人是俱乐部的会长。俱乐部最终建起了一家公共图书馆。海伦说："我写信给朋友们，以赢得他们的支持。在很短时间里，我就收到了几百本书，其中包括许多精美的好书，同时，我还收到了许多捐款和鼓励。这些慷慨的援助激励着一些女士，此后，她们坚持不懈地收集并购买了很多图书。到目前为止，镇上的公共图书馆已颇具规模。"

致查尔斯·E.英奇斯夫人

（宾夕法尼亚州希尔顿，1893年10月21日）

　　……我们在塔斯坎比亚的家中度过了九月，大家欢聚一堂……我们参观了世界博览会之后，即激动不已又疲惫不堪，所以我们那安静的山庄是个富有魅力、让人休憩的好地方。我们比以往更能体会出群山的秀丽和幽静。

　　现在我们又来到宾夕法尼亚州的希尔顿。今年冬天，我将在这里，在老师的帮助下接受一位家庭教师的补习。我要学习算术、拉丁语和文学。我很喜欢这些课程。学习新知识令我很高兴。每天我都发现自己知之甚少，但我并不气馁，因为上帝赋予了我一颗恒心，让我去学习更多的知识。在文学方面，我正在学朗费罗的诗歌。在我能区分提喻和隐喻的修辞方法之前，我就特别喜欢朗费罗的诗歌，所以我已背会了许多诗。我过去常说自己不太喜欢算术，但现在我改变想法了。我发现它是一门很好、很有用的学科。当然我也承认自己有时会心不在焉！因为和优美的诗歌或者动人的故事相比，算术精细而有用，但却有些枯燥。请为我祝福吧，光阴似箭啊！我只能用一点点时间来回答您关于"海伦·凯勒"公共图书馆的问题。

1. 我认为亚拉巴马州的塔斯坎比亚大约有3000人，其中可能有一半是有色人种。2. 现在镇上没有任何图书馆，所以我才考虑建一座。我母亲和几位闺蜜说她们愿帮助我，所以她们成立了个俱乐部，目的就是要在塔斯坎比亚建一座免费的公共图书馆。她们现在有100本左右的图书和大约55美元钱，一位善良的绅士愿意提供土地供我们建图书馆。同时，俱乐部还在镇中心租了间小房子，我们所有的书都供读者免费借阅。3. 我在波士顿的朋友只有少部分知道图书馆的事。我不想麻烦他们，因为我还在为可怜的小汤米筹款；比起让人们有书去阅读，汤米接受教育当然更为重要。4. 我不知道我们有哪些书，我认为我们收集的书是五花八门的（我想应该用这个词来形容）……

附：我的老师认为，要保存好为建设基金捐款的人员名单，并将该名单刊登在我父亲编辑的《北方阿拉巴马人报》上，这样才更务实。

H.K.

To Mrs. Charles E. Inches

Hulton, Penn., Oct. 21, 1893.

…We spent September at home in Tuscumbia … and were all very happy together … Our quiet mountain home was especially attractive and restful after the excitement and fatigue of our visit to the World's Fair. We enjoyed the beauty and solitude of the hills more than ever.

And now we are in Hulton, Penn. again where I am going to study this winter with a tutor assisted by my dear teacher. I study Arithmetic, Latin and literature. I enjoy my lessons very much. It is so pleasant to learn about new things. Every day I find how little I know, but I do not feel discouraged since God has given me an eternity in which to learn more. In literature I am studying Longfellow's poetry. I know a great deal of it by heart, for I loved it long before I knew a metaphor from a synecdoche. I used to say I did not like arithmetic very well, but now I have changed my mind. I see what a good and useful study it is, though I must confess my mind wanders from it sometimes! for, nice and useful as arithmetic is, it is not as interesting as a beautiful poem or a lovely story. But bless me, how time does fly. I have only a few moments left in which to answer your questions about the "Helen Keller" Public Library.

1. I think there are about 3,000 people in Tuscumbia, Ala., and perhaps half of them are colored people. 2. At present there is no library of any sort in the town. That is why I thought about starting one. My mother and several of my lady friends said they would help me, and they formed a club, the object of which is to work for the establishment of a free public library in Tuscumbia. They have now about 100 books and about $55 in money, and a kind gentleman has given us land on which to erect a library building. But in the meantime the club has rented a little room in a central part of the town, and the books which we already have are free to all. 3. Only a few of my kind friends in Boston know anything about the library. I did not like to trouble them while I was trying to get money for poor little Tommy; for of course it was more important that he should be educated than that my people should have books to read. 4. I do not know what books we have, but I think it is a miscellaneous (I think that is the word) collection...

P. S. My teacher thinks it would be more businesslike to say that a list of the contributors toward the building fund will be kept and published in my father's paper, the "North Alabamian."

H. K.

七

开始读唇训练

2月,海伦和沙利文小姐回到了塔斯坎比亚。整个春天,她们都在读书和学习。夏天,她们参加了"美国聋人语言教学促进协会"在肖托夸举办的会议,沙利文小姐在会上宣读了一篇关于教育海伦·凯勒的论文。

秋天,海伦和沙利文小姐进入纽约的莱特—休梅森聋人学校,那是一所在教授读唇和发音训练方面别具特色的学校。"唱歌课"加强了海伦的发声能力。她还在帕金斯学校上了几节钢琴课。这当然是非常有趣的尝试,但却以失败告终。

致卡罗琳·德比小姐

(纽约莱特—休梅森学校,1895年3月15日)

……我认为自己在读唇上有一点进步,当然对语速太快的谈话,我还是很吃力;我相信只要坚持不懈,总有一天我能成功。休梅森博士还在改进我的发音。哦,卡莉,我多么希望能像其他人一样说话啊!如果能够成功,我情愿夜以继日地练习。想想吧,如果我所有的朋友都能听见我自如地说话,那将是多么令人欢欣鼓舞的事啊!!我真想知道,为什么对聋儿来说,学说话是如此困难和难以领悟,而对正常人来说却很容易呢?但我相信,只要自己有足够的耐心,总有一天我会流利地说话的……

虽然我很忙，但我还是抽时间读了许多书……我最近读了席勒的《威廉·泰尔》[1]，以及《失落的修女》……我现在正在读莱辛的《智者纳坦》[2]和穆罗克小姐的《亚瑟王》。

……您知道，我们亲爱的老师们总是领我们看他们觉得我们会感兴趣的每件东西，通过这种寓教于乐的方式，我们愉快地学到了很多知识。在乔治·华盛顿的生日那天，我们去看了"狗狗秀"。尽管麦迪逊广场公园拥挤不堪，"狗狗管弦乐队"制造的声音令那些能听见的人们无比困惑，但那个下午我们还是玩得很高兴。在所有狗狗中，最引人注目的是斗牛犬。它们被给予了最大限度的自由。当有人爱抚它们时，它们几乎会钻进人们的胳膊里，不拘礼节地自在亲吻，而对自己不得体的举止浑然不觉。哇，斗牛犬真是丑巴巴的小东西！它们温顺而友好，人们都情不自禁地喜欢上它们了。

休梅森博士、老师和我与参观"狗狗秀"的其他人分手后，就去参加由"大都会俱乐部"主办的招待会……有时，该俱乐部也被称为"百万富翁俱乐部"。俱乐部大楼由白色大理石建造，雄伟壮观；房间很大，富丽堂皇；但我必须承认，如此奢华的场所令我感到很压抑；其实我丝毫也不妒忌这光彩夺目的场所会给百万富翁们所带来的快乐……

To Miss Caroline Derby

(*The Wright-Humason School, New York, March 15, 1895.*)

…I think I have improved a little in lip-reading, though I still find it very difficult to read rapid speech; but I am sure I shall succeed some day if I only persevere. Dr. Humason is still trying to improve my speech. Oh, Carrie, how I should like to speak like other people! I should be willing to work night

①《威廉·泰尔》是德国伟大的诗人和戏剧作家席勒的最后一部重要剧作。
②《智者纳坦》：作者为德国作家莱辛，始自《十日谈》中"三个戒指"的故事。是欧洲思想启蒙运动时期的伟大著作。

and day if it could only be accomplished. Think what a joy it would be to all of my friends to hear me speak naturally!! I wonder why it is so difficult and perplexing for a deaf child to learn to speak when it is so easy for other people; but I am sure I shall speak perfectly some time if I am only patient…

Although I have been so busy, I have found time to read a good deal…I have lately read "Wilhelm Tell" by Schiller, and "The Lost Vestal."…Now I am reading "Nathan the Wise" by Lessing and "King Arthur" by Miss Mulock.

…You know our kind teachers take us to see everything which they think will interest us, and we learn a great deal in that delightful way. On George Washington's birthday we all went to the Dog Show, and although there was a great crowd in the Madison Square Garden, and despite the bewilderment caused by the variety of sounds made by the dog-orchestra, which was very confusing to those who could hear them, we enjoyed the afternoon very much. Among the dogs which received the most attention were the bull-dogs. They permitted themselves startling liberties when any one caressed them, crowding themselves almost into one's arms and helping themselves without ceremony to kisses, apparently unconscious of the impropriety of their conduct. Dear me, what unbeautiful little beasts they are! But they are so good natured and friendly, one cannot help liking them.

Dr. Humason, Teacher, and I left the others at the Dog Show and went to a reception given by the "Metropolitan Club."…It is sometimes called the "Millionaires' Club." The building is magnificent, being built of white marble; the rooms are large and splendidly furnished; but I must confess, so much splendor is rather oppressive to me; and I didn't envy the millionaires in the least all the happiness their gorgeous surroundings are supposed to bring them…

当莱特—休梅森学校放暑假时,沙利文小姐和海伦回到了南方。从下面这封信中我们可以得知海伦对手写书信的执着。

致劳伦斯·胡顿夫人

(亚拉巴马州塔斯坎比亚,1895年7月29日)

……我正在自己那风景秀丽、阳光灿烂的家里平静而愉快地过暑假,亲爱的父母、可爱的小妹妹和小弟弟菲利普斯都跟我在一起。敬爱的老师也在我身旁,所以我当然很高兴。我每天读读书、散散步、写写字,然后跟孩子们痛痛快快地玩,日子就这么欢快地溜走啦!……

我的朋友们对我去年在说话和读唇上取得的进步感到很高兴,所以大家决定最好让我继续在纽约再学习一年,我很高兴又将在您所在的大城市里度过一年时光。以前,我曾经以为自己在纽约不会有"家"的感觉,但我却在那结识了许多人。每当我回首在纽约度过的快乐而富有成效的冬季时,我发现自己真切盼望明年的到来,还想在这座大都市领略那更加美好的时光。

请代我向胡顿先生、里格斯夫人和沃纳先生问好,虽然我还没机会亲自结识胡顿先生。每当我听到威尼斯监护人的事,我仿佛就听见了胡顿先生的钢笔在他新书上的页面上起舞的声音。这声音是多么悦耳动听呀!因为它满载着沉甸甸的承诺。我一定会津津有味地阅读这本书的!

亲爱的胡顿夫人,请原谅我,漂洋过海寄了一封打印的信给您。自从回家之后,我几次尝试用铅笔在我小写字板上写信;但天气炎热,我发现很难亲笔写信。因为我的手汗水淋漓,会把纸弄脏,模糊一片,字迹不清,所以我不得不用打字机了。这可不是我在搞"雷明顿艺术",而是因为一个淘气的小家伙在轻微刺激下出了故障而已,我不会长期这样写信的……

To Mrs. Laurence Hutton

(*Tuscumbia, Alabama, July 29, 1895.*)

…I am spending my vacation very quietly and pleasantly at my beautiful, sunny home, with my loving parents, my darling little sister and my small brother, Phillips. My precious teacher is with me too, and so of course I am happy I read a little, walk a little, write a little and play with the children a great deal, and the days slip by delightfully !…

My friends are so pleased with the improvement which I had in speech and lip-reading last year, that it has been decided best for me to continue my studies in New York another year I am delighted at the prospect of spending another year in your great city I used to think that I should never feel "at home" in New York; but since I have made the acquaintance of so many people, and can look back to such a bright and successful winter there, I find myself looking forward to next year, and anticipating still brighter and better times in the Metropolis.

Please give my kindest love to Mr Hutton, and Mrs Riggs and Mr Warner too, although I have never had the pleasure of knowing him personally. As I listen Venice-wards, I hear Mr Hutton's pen dancing over the pages of his new book It is a pleasant sound because it is full of promise How much I shall enjoy reading it !

Please pardon me, my dear Mrs Hutton, for sending you a typewritten letter across the ocean I have tried several times to write with a pencil on my little writing machine since I came home; but I have found it very difficult to do so on account of the heat The moisture of my hand soils and blurs the paper so dreadfully, that I am compelled to use my typewriter altogether And it is not my "Remington" either, but a naughty little thing that gets out of order on the slightest provocation, and cannot be induced to make a period…

海伦对读唇训练越来越有信心，幸运的是，她周围也有很多支持她的人。

致卡罗琳·德比小姐

（纽约，1895年12月29日）

……老师和我最近都过得很愉快。我们见到了好朋友道奇夫人、胡顿夫妇、里格斯夫人和她丈夫，还遇到很多了不起的名人，其中有埃伦·特里小姐、亨利·欧文爵士和斯托克顿先生！我们是不是很幸运呀？特里小姐很可爱。她亲吻老师并说："我说不清楚见到您我是不是很高兴，因为每当我想到您为这个小姑娘付出了那么多时，我就感到很惭愧。"我还遇到了特里夫妇，他们是特里小姐的哥哥和嫂子。我想特里小姐一定宛如天使一样美丽，哦，她的声音是多么清脆甜美啊！一星期前，也就是上周五，我们在戏剧《国王查理一世》[3]中，再次见到了特里小姐和亨利爵士。演出结束后，他们友好地让我触摸他们，使我对他们的长相有了一定概念。国王是多么高尚和高贵啊！特别是在他直面挫折的时候。而可怜的王后又是多么优雅和忠贞啊！表演惟妙惟肖，我们几乎忘了身在何处，虽然他们在表演很久以前的故事，我们却感觉自己看到的就像真的身临其境一样。最后一幕深深感动了我们，我们都流泪了，真不知刽子手的心为何如此残忍，竟把国王从他深爱的妻子怀抱中撕扯了出来。

我刚读完《劫后英雄传》[4]，这是本激动人心的书，但坦白地说，我不太喜欢它。可爱的瑞贝卡，具有坚强而勇敢的精神，纯洁而慷慨的

---

[3]查理一世（1600-1649），曾为英格兰、苏格兰与爱尔兰国王，是英国历史上唯一一位被处死的国王。他的死标志着英国封建专制的结束，资产阶级共和国时代的开始。

[4]《劫后英雄传》是英国作家沃尔特·司各特的名著，是一部脍炙人口的历史小说。

秉性，她是唯一一位令我钦佩的角色。现在我正在读《苏格兰历史故事集》，这本书非常惊心动魄、引人入胜！……

To Miss Caroline Derby

(*New York, December 29, 1895.*)

…Teacher and I have been very gay of late. We have seen our kind friends, Mrs. Dodge, Mr. and Mrs. Hutton, Mrs. Riggs and her husband, and met many distinguished people, among whom were Miss Ellen Terry, Sir Henry Irving and Mr. Stockton! Weren't we very fortunate? Miss Terry was lovely. She kissed Teacher and said, "I do not know whether I am glad to see you or not; for I feel so ashamed of myself when I think of how much you have done for the little girl."We also met Mr. and Mrs. Terry, Miss Terry's brother and his wife. I thought her beauty angelic, and oh, what a clear, beautiful voice she had! We saw Miss Terry again with Sir Henry in "King Charles the First, " a week ago last Friday, and after the play they kindly let me feel of them and get an idea of how they looked. How noble and kingly the King was, especially in his misfortunes! And how pretty and faithful the poor Queen was! The play seemed so real, we almost forgot where we were, and believed we were watching the genuine scenes as they were acted so long ago. The last act affected us most deeply, and we all wept, wondering how the executioner could have the heart to tear the King from his loving wife's arms.

I have just finished reading "Ivanhoe." It was very exciting; but I must say I did not enjoy it very much. Sweet Rebecca, with her strong, brave spirit and her pure, generous nature, was the only character which thoroughly won my admiration. Now I am reading"Stories from Scottish History," and they are very thrilling and absorbing!…

还记得海伦很小的时候就开始学习法语和德语词汇的书写，这一年她已能将这两种语言说得非常流利。

致卡罗琳·德比小姐

（纽约，1896年4月25日）

……我的学习照常进行，就像您上次见到我时一样，稍有不同的是，一位法语老师开始教我法语，每周来三次。我几乎只能靠读唇的方式来学习（她不懂手语字母），我们相处得很好。我已愉快地读了《屈打成医》⑤，这是莫里哀写的一部法国喜剧；老师们说我现在法语说得很好，德语也说得不错。不管怎样，法国人和德国人都能听懂我想说的话了，这真令人欢欣鼓舞。在语音训练方面，我面临的还是老问题；看来，要实现流利说话的可能性似乎为零，简直是遥不可及啊！有时我觉得自己隐约瞥见了追求的目标；可是下一刻，路上的一个弯道却把这目标隐匿在了我的视线之外，我又在黑暗中徘徊！但我决不言弃。坚信我们最终都能实现自己的理想……

To Miss Caroline Derby

(*New York, April 25, 1896.*)

…My studies are the same as they were when I saw you, except that I have taken up French with a French teacher who comes three times a week. I read her lips almost exclusively, (she does not know the manual alphabet) and we get on quite well. I have read "Le Médecin Malgré Lui," a very good French comedy by Molière, with pleasure; and they say I speak French pretty well now, and German also. Anyway, French and German people understand what I am trying to say, and that is very encouraging. In voice-training I have still the same old difficulties to contend against; and the fulfilment of my wish

---

⑤《屈打成医》：法国喜剧作家、演员、戏剧活动家莫里哀的著名话剧。

to speak well seems O, so far away! Sometimes I feel sure that I catch a faint glimpse of the goal I am striving for; but in another minute a bend in the road hides it from my view, and I am again left wandering in the dark! But I try hard not to be discouraged. Surely we shall all find at last the ideals we are seeking…

致约翰·希茨先生

（马萨诸塞州布鲁斯特，1896年7月15日）

……当我在老师那灵巧而神奇的手指的指引下，走进那本书时，我就深信自己会喜欢它的；我已和去不老泉的两姐妹变成了好伙伴。

我正坐在窗边给您写信，轻柔而凉爽的和风吹拂着我的脸颊，我感觉去年的艰苦工作已经结束啦！老师看起来也得益于这种变化；她开始回复到从前的自我了。我们只需要您，亲爱的希茨先生，使我们的幸福更加圆满。老师和霍普金斯夫人都说您必须尽快过来！我们会让您感到舒适而温馨的。

老师和我在费城待了九天。您曾去过克劳特博士研究院吗？可能豪斯先生已经给您了一份我们的做事清单。我们一直很忙，忙于参加会议；和许许多多的人交谈，其中有尊敬的贝尔博士、加尔各答的班纳吉先生、巴黎的马尼亚先生和其他许多著名人士，我已可以用法语单独跟马尼亚先生交谈了。我们真希望能在费城见到您，所以您没来令我们感到很遗憾。我们时刻想念您！我们的心满怀深情与您相伴。这封信会告诉您，并让您更好地了解我们和您在一起时是多么快乐！7月8日，我做了一次"演讲"，告诉协会的成员们，学会说话对我来说是一种无以言表的幸福，并敦促他们给每一个聋儿一个学习说话的机会。大家都认为我讲得清晰易懂。在我的小型"演讲"结束后，我们参加了一个有600多人出席的招待会。坦白地说，我不喜欢这么大型的招待会；人员拥挤不堪，

我们不得不说个不停；但是，也只有在像费城这样的招待会上，我们才能经常遇到日后会逐渐喜欢的朋友。上星期四晚上我们离开了费城，于星期五下午到达布鲁斯特。我们错过了星期五早上去鳕鱼角的火车，所以我们坐蒸汽船"朗费罗"号到达了普罗温斯敦，此次旅行令我很高兴；在水上航行愉快而凉爽，波士顿港也总是魅力无穷。

离开纽约后，我们在波士顿待了三个星期。毋庸赘述，我们过得很愉快。我们拜访了好友张伯伦夫妇，他们在伦瑟姆的乡村有个温馨的家。他们的房子伫立在一个美丽的湖边，我们在湖上划船、玩独木舟，开心极了。我们还游了几次泳。6月17日，张伯伦夫妇在为他们的文学界朋友举办了野餐庆祝会。约有40人出席，他们都是作家和出版商。我们的朋友、《竖琴师》的编辑奥尔登先生也来了，能跟他见面，我们当然欣喜万分。

To Mr. John Hitz

(*Brewster, Mass. July 15, 1896.*)

…As to the book, I am sure I shall enjoy it very much when I am admitted, by the magic of Teacher's dear fingers, into the companionship of the two sisters who went to the Immortal Fountain.

As I sit by the window writing to you, it is so lovely to have the soft, cool breezes fan my cheek, and to feel that the hard work of last year is over! Teacher seems to feel benefited by the change too; for she is already beginning to look like her dear old self. We only need you, dear Mr. Hitz, to complete our happiness. Teacher and Mrs. Hopkins both say you *must* come as soon as you can! We will try to make you comfortable.

Teacher and I spent nine days at Philadelphia. Have you ever been at Dr. Crouter's Institution? Mr. Howes has probably given you a full account of our doings. We were busy all the time; we attended the meetings and talked with hundreds of people, among whom were dear Dr. Bell, Mr. Banerji of Calcutta, Monsieur Magnat of Paris with whom I conversed in French exclusively, and many other distinguished persons. We had looked forward to seeing you there, and so we were greatly disappointed that you did not come. We think of you so, so often! And our hearts go out to you in tenderest sympathy; and you know better than this poor letter can tell you how happy we always are to have you with us! I made a "speech" on July eighth, telling the members of the Association what an unspeakable blessing speech has been to me, and urging them to give every little deaf child an opportunity to learn to speak. Every one said I spoke very well and intelligibly. After my little "speech," we attended a reception at which over six hundred people were present. I must confess I do not like such large receptions; the people crowd so, and we have to do so much talking; and yet it is at receptions like the one in Philadelphia that we often meet friends whom we learn to love afterwards. We left the city last Thursday night, and arrived in Brewster Friday afternoon. We missed the Cape Cod train Friday morning, and so we came down to Provincetown in the steamer *Longfellow*, I am glad we did so; for it was lovely and cool on the water, and Boston Harbor is always interesting.

  We spent about three weeks in Boston, after leaving New York, and I need not tell you we had a most delightful time. We visited our good friends, Mr. and Mrs. Chamberlin, at Wrentham, out in the country, where they have a lovely home. Their house stands near a charming lake where we went boating and canoeing, which was great fun. We also went in bathing several times. Mr. and Mrs. Chamberlin celebrated the 17th of June by giving a picnic to their literary friends. There were about forty persons present, all of whom were writers and publishers. Our friend, Mr. Alden, the editor of *Harper*'s was there, and of course we enjoyed his society very much…

八

圆大学之梦

1896年10月1日，海伦进入剑桥青年女子学校学习，亚瑟·吉尔曼先生是该校校长。下面信里提到的"考试"，只是该校的测验，但由于试题是哈佛学院以前的考卷，可见，海伦为了进入拉德克利夫学院，在一些科目上显然已做了充分的准备。

致劳伦斯·胡顿夫人

（马萨诸塞州剑桥康科德大街37号，1896年10月8日）

……今天早上我起得很早，所以我可以给您写几行字。我知道您想听听我对学校的看法。我真希望您也能亲自来看看这是一所多么美丽的学校啊！这里大约有100名女生，她们聪颖而快乐，能跟她们在一起真是一种幸福。

当您知道我成功地通过了考试，一定会很高兴的。我参加了英语、德语、法语、希腊语和罗马历史的考试。这些试卷都是哈佛学院的入学考卷，所以我很高兴自己能通过考试。今年对老师和我来说都会是很忙的一年。我正在学算术、英国文学、英语、历史、德语、拉丁语和高级地理，还要进行大量的预习阅读。由于只有少量的书有盲文版，所以可怜的老师不得不把书中的内容——拼写给我；这是一项十分艰巨的工作。

当您见到豪厄尔斯先生时，请一定要告诉他我们住在他的房子里……

To Mrs. Laurence Hutton

(*37 Concord Avenue, Cambridge, Mass. October 8, 1896.*)

…I got up early this morning, so that I could write you a few lines. I know you want to hear how I like my school. I do wish you could come and see for yourself what a beautiful school it is! There are about a hundred girls, and they are all so bright and happy; it is a joy to be with them.

You will be glad to hear that I passed my examinations successfully. I have been examined in English, German, French, and Greek and Roman history. They were the entrance examinations for Harvard College; so I feel pleased to think I could pass them. This year is going to be a very busy one for Teacher and myself. I am studying Arithmetic, English Literature, English, History, German, Latin, and advanced geography; there is a great deal of preparatory reading required, and, as few of the books are in raised print, poor Teacher has to spell them all out to me; and that means hard work.

You must tell Mr. Howells when you see him, that we are living in his house…

1898年，由于吉尔曼先生的干涉，导致凯勒夫人让凯勒小姐和她的妹妹米尔德丽德从剑桥学校退学。沙利文小姐和她的学生去了伦瑟姆，在一位热情洋溢且经验丰富的老师——默顿·S.基思先生的辅导下学习。

致劳伦斯·胡顿夫人

（马萨诸塞州伦瑟姆，1898年2月20日）

……您离开后我继续学习，有短暂的一段时间我们学得很愉

快，仿佛一个月前的可怕经历只是一个梦。我无法向您讲述我对乡村的喜爱之情。这里是如此清新、宁静和自由！如果允许的话，我觉得自己可以孜孜不倦地学习一整天。这有许多令人愉快的事可以做——但可不都是简单的事——我觉得代数和几何就很难；但我喜欢所有的功课，特别是希腊语。想想吧，我快学完语法喽！接着就要学《伊利亚特》。一想到自己很快就能用那光辉灿烂的希腊语读懂阿喀琉斯①、尤利西斯、安德洛玛刻②、雅典娜③和其他老朋友的故事了，我真是欣喜若狂！我认为希腊语是我所知道的最优美的语言。如果小提琴是最完美的乐器，那么希腊语就是人类语言中的小提琴。

这个月我们还滑了几次雪橇。每天早晨上课前，我们都要到房子旁、湖北岸陡峭的山上，滑行一个小时左右。有人在山顶上让雪橇保持平衡，当我们坐上雪橇，准备好之后，雪橇就带着我们沿着山腰飞驰而下，越过小坡，穿出雪堆，以惊人的速度飞越池塘！

To Mrs. Laurence Hutton

(*Wrentham, Mass., February 20, 1898.*)

…I resumed my studies soon after your departure, and in a very little while we were working as merrily as if the dreadful experience of a month ago had been but a dream. I cannot tell you how much I enjoy the country. It is so fresh, and peaceful and free! I do think I could work all day long without feeling tired if they would let me. There are so many pleasant things to do—not always very

---

①阿喀琉斯是荷马史诗《伊利亚特》中参加特洛伊战争的一个半神英雄，希腊联军第一勇士。因被太阳神阿波罗一箭射中了脚踝而死去，后人常以"阿喀琉斯之踵"比喻英雄的死穴或软肋。

②安德洛玛刻是希腊传说中的一个女子，温柔善良，勇敢聪敏，以钟爱丈夫著称。

③雅典娜，古希腊宗教和神话中的智慧与技艺女神。

easy things, —much of my work in Algebra and Geometry is hard: but I love it all, especially Greek. Just think, I shall soon finish my grammar! Then comes the "Iliad." What an inexpressible joy it will be to read about Achilles, and Ulysses, and Andromache and Athene, and the rest of my old friends in their own glorious language! I think Greek is the loveliest language that I know anything about. If it is true that the violin is the most perfect of musical instruments, then Greek is the violin of human thought.

We have had some splendid toboganning this month. Every morning, before lesson-time, we all go out to the steep hill on the northern shore of the lake near the house, and coast for an hour or so. Some one balances the toboggan on the very crest of the hill, while we get on, and when we are ready, off we dash down the side of the hill in a headlong rush, and, leaping a projection, plunge into a snow-drift and go skimming far across the pond at a tremendous rate!

10月，凯勒小姐和沙利文小姐回到波士顿开始新阶段的阅读与学习，继续为拉德克利夫学院的入学考试做准备。这一段时间，凯勒的阅读量急剧增加，她的书信中充满了哲学性的宏大思考。这是少女凯勒思想走向成熟的重要阶段。

致劳伦斯·胡顿夫人

（波士顿纽伯里街12号，1898年10月23日）

自从我们上周一到这里之后，我第一次有机会给您写信。在我们决定来波士顿之后，我们就陷入了一连串的事务之中；似乎有做不完的工作。可怜的老师忙得不可开交，要跟搬家工人、快递员和各种各样的人们打交道。因为我们不得不经常搬家，所以我真希望搬家不要这么麻烦！……

……除了星期六，基恩先生每天三点半都会过来。他说自己目前很愿意来我们这里。我正在读《伊利亚特》《埃涅伊德》和西赛罗的作品，此外，还要花很多精力学习代数和几何。《伊利亚特》史料翔实、语言优美、朴素自然，像一个天真活泼的孩子。而《埃涅伊德》的语言则雕饰华丽，音律严谨。像一位美丽的少女，一直生活在深宫里，被华丽的庭院包围着。我觉得《伊利亚特》也像个活力四射的青年，他把地球看作了自己的操场。

整整一星期，天气都阴沉沉的；但今天天气很好，我们房间的地板上洒满了阳光。晚些时候，我们要去公园散散步。我真希望伦瑟姆的树木就在拐角处！但是，哎呀！这些树并不是那里的，我只能在花园里走走，聊以自慰。不知怎的，相比乡间那无垠的田野和牧场，以及巍峨的松树林，这里的树似乎都被禁锢了，显得迂腐而陈旧，尽管它们仿佛颇具都市气概，并充满了自我意识。事实上，我简直怀疑它们跟那些不习惯城市生活的乡巴佬们是否只是泛泛之交！我曾情不自禁地为这些气质浮华的树而感到遗憾，您知道这点吗？它们就像一些它们天天见到的人一样，宁愿待在拥挤而聒噪的城市，而不愿到宁静而自由的乡村。他们对自己生活所受的制约浑然不觉。他们看不起乡下人，觉得他们很可怜，从来没机会"去见识大世界"。哦，天哪！如果他们能意识到自己的狭隘，他们将会逃向森林和田野里去生活的。但这不过是毫无意义的废话罢了！也许您会认为我在为自己所热爱的伦瑟姆感到悲哀，从某种意义上来说，这既有对的一面，又有不对的一面。我的确十分想念瑞德农场和那些亲爱的朋友们；但我在这里也并未感到不快，因为这里不但有我的老师和书籍，而且我确信在这个大城市，我能接触到一些美好而愉快的事物。人们在这里勇敢地奋斗，从残酷的环境中汲取快乐。无论如何，我都很高兴自己也能分享那些幸福的或悲惨的生活……

To Mrs. Laurence Hutton

(*12 Newbury Street, Boston, October 23, 1898.*)

This is the first opportunity I have had to write to you since we came here last Monday. We have been in such a whirl ever since we decided to come to Boston; it seemed as if we should never get settled. Poor Teacher has had her hands full, attending to movers, and expressmen, and all sorts of people. I wish it were not such a bother to move, especially as we have to do it so often!…

…Mr. Keith comes here at half past three every day except Saturday. He says he prefers to come here for the present. I am reading the "Iliad." and the "Aeneid" and Cicero, besides doing a lot in Geometry and Algebra. The "Iliad" is beautiful with all the truth, and grace and simplicity of a wonderfully childlike people while the "Aeneid" is more stately and reserved. It is like a beautiful maiden, who always lived in a palace, surrounded by a magnificent court; while the "Iliad" is like a splendid youth, who has had the earth for his playground.

The weather has been awfully dismal all the week; but to-day is beautiful, and our room floor is flooded with sunlight. By and by we shall take a little walk in the Public Gardens. I wish the Wrentham woods were round the corner! But alas! they are not, and I shall have to content myself with a stroll in the Gardens. Somehow, after the great fields and pastures and lofty pinegroves of the country, they seem shut-in and conventional. Even the trees seem citified and self-conscious. Indeed, I doubt if they are on speaking terms with their country cousins! Do you know, I cannot help feeling sorry for these trees with all their fashionable airs? They are like the people whom they see every day, who prefer the crowded, noisy city to the quiet and freedom of the country. They do not even suspect how circumscribed their lives are. They look down pityingly on the countryfolk, who have never had an opportunity "to see the great world." Oh my! if they only realized their limitations, they would flee for their lives to the woods and fields. But what nonsense is this! You will think I'm pining away for my beloved Wrentham, which is true in one sense and not in another. I do miss Red Farm and the dear ones there dreadfully; but I am not unhappy. I have Teacher and my books, and I have the certainty that something sweet and good will come to me in this great city, where human beings struggle so bravely all their lives to wring happiness from cruel circumstances. Anyway, I am glad to have my share in life, whether it be bright or sad…

致劳伦斯·胡顿夫人

(波士顿纽伯里街12号，1899年1月17日)

……您曾看过吉卜林的《美梦成真》，或是《基奇纳的学校》吗？这些诗歌铿锵有力，令我无比神往。当然，您已经读过有关"戈登纪念学院"[4]的资料了，那是英国人民在喀土穆建的学院。我在想，福祉会通过这所学院传达给埃及人民，最终又会返回给英国人民。我心里有个强烈愿望，我亲爱的祖国也应该仿效这种方式，虽然"缅因号"军舰爆炸事件[5]损失惨重，令美国失去了许多勇敢的战士，但也可以把这件事

---

④1902年，基奇纳勋爵为纪念戈登将军，在苏丹首都喀土穆的市中心建立了戈登学院，它是苏丹最早建立的高等学府，也曾是非洲排名第一的大学，1951年正式命名为喀土穆大学。

⑤1898年2月15日晚，美国战舰"缅因号"在古巴哈瓦那港外突然爆炸沉没，260多名水手葬身海底。事件发生后，美国海军认为是西班牙人用水雷炸沉了"缅因号"，在煽动起来的民意支持下，美国向西班牙宣战，结果不仅一举击败这个老牌帝国，还一跃成为势力范围囊括拉美和亚洲的新兴世界强国。

转化为对古巴人民的美好祝福。在哈瓦那建一所学院不就等于是给"缅因号"的勇士们树立了一座永垂不朽的纪念碑吗？它是不是还能成为相关各方无穷的善意之源呢？可以想象一下：当您乘船驶入哈瓦那港，有人指着那个码头告诉您，在那个月黑风高之夜，"缅因号"就抛锚停泊在该码头，她在此被神秘地摧毁了。但同时，人们还指着一栋巍峨雄壮、俯瞰码头的建筑物告诉您，那就是"缅因纪念学院"，这是美国人民为了让古巴人和西班牙人接受教育而建立的！诚如斯哉，那么这座纪念学院，将会是一个多么辉煌的胜利象征啊！同时，它也将是一个基督教民族最善良、最高尚的天性的体现！在这里，将没有仇恨或报复，陈旧的观念也没有立足之地。此外，它还是我们给世界的一个承诺，我们将信守战争宣言，当我们觉得古巴人民能够担当起人民自治的责任和义务时，我们就会把古巴交还给古巴人民……

To Mrs. Laurence Hutton

(*12 Newbury Street, Boston, January 17, 1899.*)

…Have you seen Kipling's "Dreaming True,"or "Kitchener's school?" It is a very strong poem and set me dreaming too. Of course you have read about the "Gordon Memorial College," which the English people are to erect at Khartoum. While I was thinking over the blessings that would come to the people of Egypt through this college, and eventually to England herself, there came into my heart the strong desire that my own dear country should in a similar way convert the terrible loss of her brave sons on the "Maine" into a like blessing to the people of Cuba. Would a college at Havana not be the noblest and most enduring monument that could be raised to the brave men of the "Maine," as well as a source of infinite good to all concerned? Imagine entering the Havana harbor, and having the pier, where the "Maine" was anchored on that dreadful night, when she was so mysteriously destroyed, pointed out to you, and being told that the great, beautiful building overlooking the spot was the "Maine Memorial College," erected by the American people, and having for its object the education both of Cubans and Spaniards! What a glorious triumph such a monument would be of the best and highest instincts of a Christian nation! In it there would be no suggestion of hatred or revenge, nor a trace of the old-time belief that might makes right. On the other hand, it would be a pledge to the world that we intend to stand by our declaration of war, and give Cuba to the Cubans, as soon as we have fitted them to assume the duties and responsibilities of a self-governing people…

致约翰·希茨先生

（波士顿纽伯里街12号，1899年2月3日）

……上周一，我参加了一项妙趣横生的活动。那天早上，一位好友带我去波士顿艺术博物馆参观。她事先从博物馆主管洛林将军那得到了特别许可，允许我触摸雕塑，特别是触摸那些表现《伊利亚特》和《埃涅伊德》中我熟识得像老朋友一样的人物的作品。这是不是很让人很开心呀？我到那里时，洛林将军也亲自来到博物馆，向我展示了一些最精湛的雕塑，其中有梅第奇的维纳斯像⑥、巴台农神庙的密涅瓦（掌管智慧、工艺和战争的女神），还有黛安娜。黛安娜身穿狩猎服，手扶箭筒，一只母鹿站在她身旁。还有不幸的拉奥孔⑦和他的两个小儿子的雕像，两

⑥维纳斯是罗马神话中的爱神与美神，同时又是执掌生育与航海的女神。古希腊神话中称为阿芙罗狄蒂。

⑦拉奥孔雕像为大理石群雕，高约184厘米，创作于约公元前一世纪，现收藏于罗马梵蒂冈美术馆。被推崇为世上最完美的作品。

条凶恶的巨蛇缠住了他们，他们正奋力挣扎，手臂绝望地伸向天空，同时撕心裂肺地哭喊着。我还看见了观景殿的阿波罗[8]，他刚刚杀死了巨蟒，正站在一根巨大的石柱旁，因为战胜了可怕的巨蟒而挥舞着他强健的手臂。哦，他是多么率真而英俊啊！维纳斯也让我着迷，她看上去仿佛刚刚从泛着细波的海里升起来，美得宛如一段天籁之音。我还看见了可怜的尼俄柏[9]，她紧紧搂着一个最小的幼女，乞求残暴的女神不要杀死她最后的一个孩子。这雕像非常凄惨而逼真，以至于我都几乎要哭了。洛林将军还友好地给我们看了佛罗伦萨圣若望洗礼堂精美铜门的复制品，我还触摸了优雅的门柱，在凶猛的狮子背上小憩。所以您看，将来有一天我希望能去参观佛罗伦萨，但我已提前体会了个中趣味。我的朋友说，有机会的话，她会带我去看埃尔金王从巴台农神庙带回来的大理石雕像的复制品。但从我的内心深处来说，我更愿意去原址看真品，是神灵让它们成了遗迹。它们既是一首对诸神的赞美诗，又是一座光辉希腊的纪念碑。而把这些神圣的物品从它们所属的古老圣殿里抢走，这似乎真是一个错误……

To Mr. John Hitz

(*12 Newbury Street, Boston, February 3, 1899.*)

…I had an exceedingly interesting experience last Monday. A kind friend took me over in the morning to the Boston Art Museum. She had previously obtained permission from General Loring, Supt. of the Museum, for me to touch the statues, especially those which represented my old friends in the "Iliad" and "Aeneid." Was that not lovely? While I was

---

[8]观景殿的阿波罗是一尊白色大理石古代雕塑，高2.24米，由希腊雕塑家莱奥卡雷斯完成于公元前350年到前325年，在15世纪文艺复兴时期被重新发现。

[9]大理石复制品，高149厘米，现收藏于罗马国立美术馆，原作为斯珂帕斯创作于约公元前4世纪。堪称是古典现实主义艺术的典范之一。

there, General Loring himself came in, and showed me some of the most beautiful statues, among which were the Venus of Medici, the Minerva of the Parthenon, Diana, in her hunting costume, with her hand on the quiver and a doe by her side, and the unfortunate Laocoön and his two little sons, struggling in the fearful coils of two huge serpents, and stretching their arms to the skies with heart-rending cries. I also saw Apollo Belvidere. He had just slain the Python and was standing by a great pillar of rock, extending his graceful hand in triumph over the terrible snake. Oh, he was simply beautiful! Venus entranced me. She looked as if she had just risen from the foam of the sea, and her loveliness was like a strain of heavenly music. I also saw poor Niobe with her youngest child clinging close to her while she implored the cruel goddess not to kill her last darling. I almost cried, it was all so real and tragic. General Loring kindly showed me a copy of one of the wonderful bronze doors of the Baptistry of Florence, and I felt of the graceful pillars, resting on the backs of fierce lions. So you see, I had a foretaste of the pleasure which I hope some day to have of visiting Florence. My friend said, she would sometime show me the copies of the marbles brought away by Lord Elgin from the Parthenon. But somehow, I should prefer to see the originals in the place where Genius meant them to remain, not only as a hymn of praise to the gods, but also as a monument of the glory of Greece. It really seems wrong to snatch such sacred things away from the sanctuary of the Past where they belong…

致威廉·韦德先生

（波士顿，1899年2月19日）

哦，祝福您！在我收到《牧歌集》[10]之后，就赶紧给您写信，想告诉您能拥有这些书，令我多么快乐！也许您从未收到过那封信，但不管怎样，亲爱的朋友，我都非常感谢您尽心尽力为我所做的一切。当您听到来自英国的书籍已寄到时，您应该会开心的。我已有《埃涅伊德》的第七册和第八册书，还有一本《伊利亚特》。正好我的盲文版课本差不多全部都要读完了，所以能拥有这些书真是太幸运了。

每当我听到针对聋盲人已经开展了许多工作时，我就非常高兴。随着我对他们的进一步了解，我发现他们有许多善良之处。唉！不久前人们还认为聋盲人是不可能学会什么东西的，但事实证明，千千万万颗充满善意和同情的心，都饱含着要帮助他们的意愿。现在我们可以看到，那些贫穷而不幸的人们被教导去感知生活的美好和真实。爱心总能找到通往一颗被囚禁的灵魂的道路，并引领它走向自由而智慧的世界。

至于"双手手语字母法"，我认为对于那些能看得见的人来说，它比手语字母要容易得多，因为里面的大多数字母看起来就像书中的大写字母；但我认为，如果是教聋盲人拼写，则用手语字母更方便些，也不那么显眼……

To Mr. William Wade

(*Boston, February 19th, 1899.*)

Why, bless you, I thought I wrote to you the day after the "Eclogues" arrived, and told you how glad I was to have them! Perhaps you never got that letter. At any rate, I thank you, dear friend, for taking such a world of trouble

---

[10]《牧歌集》是古罗马诗人维吉尔的代表性作品。长达10章，被认为是拉丁语文学的典范之作，有着古罗马的田园诗色彩。

for me. You will be glad to hear that the books from England are coming now. I already have the seventh and eighth books of the "Aeneid" and one book of the "Iliad," all of which is most fortunate, as I have come almost to the end of my embossed textbooks.

It gives me great pleasure to hear how much is being done for the deaf-blind. The more I learn of them, the more kindness I find. Why, only a little while ago people thought it quite impossible to teach the deaf-blind anything; but no sooner was it proved possible than hundreds of kind, sympathetic hearts were fired with the desire to help them, and now we see how many of those poor, unfortunate persons are being taught to see the beauty and reality of life. Love always finds its way to an imprisoned soul, and leads it out into the world of freedom and intelligence!

As to the two-handed alphabet, I think it is much easier for those who have sight than the manual alphabet; for most of the letters look like the large capitals in books; but I think when it comes to teaching a deaf-blind person to spell, the manual alphabet is much more convenient, and less conspicuous…

致劳伦斯·胡顿夫人

（波士顿纽伯里街12号，1899年3月5日）

……现在我确定，我要为六月份的考试做准备。目前我的天空中只有一片云，但正是这片云，却在我的生活中投下了阴影，这使我有时很着急。我老师的眼睛还没好，尽管老师勇敢而隐忍，从不言弃，但实际上我认为她眼睛的病症已加重了。每当我想到她是为了我而牺牲了自己的视力时，我就非常难过。我甚至觉得自己似乎应该彻底放弃上大学的念头。因为如果获取知识要付出这么大的代价，那么就算得到了世上所有的知识，我也不会快乐的。我真心希望，胡顿夫人，请您尽力说服老师休息一段时间，去治疗她的眼睛。她可不会听我的话。

我刚刚照了一些相片，如果它们照得不错，而您又觉得罗杰斯先生会愿意要的话，那么我想寄一张给他。我非常想用某种方式来表达我对他深深的感激之情，感谢他为我所做的一切，我实在想不出还能用什么更好的方法来回报他了。

这里的人们都在谈论萨金特⑪的画展，大家说这是一个非常精彩的肖像画展。我多么希望自己也能亲眼看看这些画啊！它们的美丽和色彩一定会使我无比欢愉！令我开心的是，我并非丝毫也不能感受到这些画所蕴含的快乐。通过朋友的眼睛，我至少也心满意足地欣赏了这些画，这是真正的快乐。我心存感激，深知自己之所以也能够享受美，是因为我的朋友们收集了美，并放入了我手中！

吉卜林先生并没有死！这真令我们高兴并感谢上苍。我有他的盲文版《丛林故事》⑫，这是一本多么美妙且令人耳目一新的书啊！我情不自禁地觉得自己仿佛认识这书的天才作者似的。他一定有着率真、充满男子汉气概的可爱性格！……

To Mrs. Laurence Hutton

(12 Newberry Street, Boston, March 5, 1899)

…I am now sure that I shall be ready for my examinations in June. There is but one cloud in my sky at present; but that is one which casts a dark shadow over my life, and makes me very anxious at times. My teacher's eyes are no

---

⑪萨金特（1856—1925），美国肖像画家。主要作品有《列布尔斯台尔爵士像》和《温汉姐妹图》等。

⑫《丛林故事》是20世纪初英国著名作家鲁德亚德·吉卜林的早期代表作，亦为其最有影响和最受欢迎的作品。

better: indeed, I think they grow more troublesome, though she is very brave and patient, and will not give up. But it is most distressing to me to feel that she is sacrificing her sight for me. I feel as if I ought to give up the idea of going to college altogether: for not all the knowledge in the world could make me happy, if obtained at such a cost. I do wish, Mrs. Hutton, you would try to persuade Teacher to take a rest, and have her eyes treated. She will not listen to me.

I have just had some pictures taken, and if they are good, I would like to send one to Mr. Rogers, if you think he would like to have it. I would like so much to show him in some way how deeply I appreciate all that he is doing for me, and I cannot think of anything better to do.

Every one here is talking about the Sargent pictures. It is a wonderful exhibition of portraits, they say. How I wish I had eyes to see them! How I should delight in their beauty and color! However, I am glad that I am not debarred from all pleasure in the pictures. I have at least the satisfaction of seeing them through the eyes of my friends, which is a real pleasure. I am so thankful that I can rejoice in the beauties, which my friends gather and put into my hands!

We are all so glad and thankful that Mr. Kipling did not die! I have his "Jungle-Book" in raised print, and what a splendid, refreshing book it is! I cannot help feeling as if I knew its gifted author. What a real, manly, lovable nature his must be!…

致大卫·H·格瑞尔博士

（波士顿纽伯里街12号，1899年5月8日）

……每个白天，我都在竭尽全力地奋斗；每个夜晚，我好好休息，同时美美地想着自己离目标又近了一步。我的希腊语进步得很快，我已经读完了第九册《伊利亚特》，正开始读《奥德赛》⑬。同时，我还在读《埃涅伊德》和《牧歌集》。有些朋友说我在希腊语和拉丁语上花那么多时间，实在是太傻了；但如果他们能意识到荷马和维吉尔为我展现了一个有着多么超凡经历和奇妙思想的世界，那么我敢肯定他们会改变想法的。《伊利亚特》讲的尽是战争，几乎没写别的。但有时枪矛刺耳的撞击声和战役的喧嚣声也会令人厌倦。而我认为自己最喜欢的是《奥德赛》，它讲的则是高贵的勇气——饱经沧桑的一颗心灵，如何历经艰险，坚定不移，最终迎来了胜利。每当我阅读这些灿烂的史诗时，我总想知道为什么荷马的战争之歌能使希腊人满怀勇猛激情，但同时他那男子汉的美德之歌为什么却不能对人们的精神生活产生较大影响呢？也许原因在于：真正伟大的思想就像撒在人们头脑里的种子，有的默默无闻地留在那里；有的则像玩具一样被玩耍、被抛掷；它们历经磨难而变得睿智，直到某个民族发现了它们，并精心培育它们。这样，世界在朝向天国的进程中才又前进了一步。

现在，我孜孜不倦地学习。我计划在六月参加考试。为此，我还要做出许多努力，才能迎接这严峻的考验。

我母亲、小妹妹和小弟弟会来北方和我一起度过这个夏天，听到这个消息您也会很高兴吧。我们会住在伦瑟姆湖边的一座小农舍里。在这里，我亲爱的老师可以好好休养一下。想想吧，12年来，她从未休过假，她一直是我生命中的阳光。目前，她深受眼疾的折磨，我们都觉得她应该放松一些，卸下所有的牵挂和责任。但我们不能完全分开，我希望我们还能每天见面。当七月来临，您想起我时，我正坐在您送给我的小船里，和亲人们一起泛舟美丽的湖上呢，我可真是世上最快乐的女孩呀！……

⑬《奥德赛》是古希腊最重要的两部史诗之一（另一部是《伊利亚特》，统称《荷马史诗》）。这部史诗是西方文学的奠基之作。

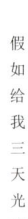

To Dr. David H. Greer

(*12 Newberry Street, Boston, May 8, 1899.*)

…Each day brings me all that I can possibly accomplish, and each night brings me rest, and the sweet thought that I am a little nearer to my goal than ever before. My Greek progresses finely. I have finished the ninth book of the "Iliad" and am just beginning the "Odyssey." I am also reading the "Aeneid" and the "Eclogues." Some of my friends tell me that I am very foolish to give so much time to Greek and Latin; but I am sure they would not think so, if they realized what a wonderful world of experience and thought Homer and Virgil have opened up to me. I think I shall enjoy the "Odyssey" most of all. The "Iliad" tells of almost nothing but war, and one sometimes wearies of the clash of spears and the din of battle, but the "Odyssey" tells of nobler courage—the courage of a soul sore tried, but steadfast to the end. I often wonder, as I read these splendid poems why, at the same time that Homer's songs of war fired the Greeks with valor, his songs of manly virtue did not have a stronger influence upon the spiritual life of the people. Perhaps the reason is, that thoughts truly great are like seeds cast into the human mind, and either lie there unnoticed, or are tossed about and played with, like toys, until grown wise through suffering and experience, a race discovers and cultivates them. Then the world has advanced one step in its heavenward march.

I am working very hard just now. I intend to take my examinations in June, and there is a great deal to be done, before I shall feel ready to meet the ordeal…

You will be glad to hear that my mother, and little sister and brother are coming north to spend this summer with me. We shall all live together in a small cottage on one, of the lakes at Wrentham, while my dear teacher takes a much needed rest. She has not had a vacation for twelve years, think of it, and all that time she has been the sunshine of my life. Now her eyes are troubling her a great deal, and we all think she ought to be relieved, for a while, of every care and responsibility. But we shall not be quite separated; we shall see each other every day, I hope. And, when July comes, you can think of me as rowing my dear ones around the lovely lake in the little boat you gave me, the happiest girl in the world!…

致劳伦斯·胡顿夫人

（波士顿，1899年5月28日）

……我们度过了艰苦的一天。基思先生今天下午在这里待了三个小时，他把拉丁语和希腊语的急流一股脑儿地倾倒在我那可怜的、茫然不知所措的大脑里。我相信他知道的拉丁语和希腊语语法简直比西塞罗[14]或荷马梦寐以求的还要多！西塞罗虽然倍受众人推崇，但他的演讲却极难翻译。有时我也感到羞愧，因为我会把这位能言善辩的演说家的话译得杂乱无章且枯燥无味；但一个学生妹又如何能诠释这样的天才呢？唉！我不得不也成为一名雄辩家，而且还要像西塞罗一样讲话……

To Mrs. Laurence Hutton

(*Boston, May 28th, 1899*).

…We have had a hard day. Mr. Keith was here for three hours this afternoon, pouring a torrent of Latin and Greek into my poor bewildered brain. I really believe he knows more Latin and Greek Grammar than Cicero or

---

[14] 马库斯·图留斯·西塞罗（公元前106年－公元前43年），古罗马著名政治家、演说家、雄辩家、法学家和哲学家。

Homer ever dreamed of! Cicero is splendid, but his orations are very difficult to translate. I feel ashamed sometimes, when I make that eloquent man say what sounds absurd or insipid; but how is a schoolgirl to interpret such genius? Why, I should have to be a Cicero to talk like a Cicero!…

  林妮·哈桂伍德是一名盲聋女孩，也是威廉·韦德先生曾帮助过的人之一。多拉·唐纳德小姐是她的老师，在唐纳德小姐对她的学生开展教学活动之初，经费是由沃尔塔办事处的主管希茨先生资助的，他还向她们提供了沙利文小姐对凯勒小姐的教学资料。

致威廉·韦德先生

（马萨诸塞州伦瑟姆，1899年6月5日）

  ……我对您几个星期以前寄给我的有关林妮·哈桂伍德的信很感兴趣。信中表现了她天真自然的可爱性格。我被她关于历史的说法逗乐了。她不喜欢历史，对此我感到遗憾，但有时我也觉得那些有关古人、古老宗教和古老政府体制的历史确实非常黑暗、神秘，甚至很可怕。

  嗯，我必须承认，我不喜欢手势语，也不认为它对盲聋人会有多大用处。我觉得很难跟上聋哑人所做的飞快动作，另外，似乎手势对盲聋人获得自如使用语言的能力也是一个巨大障碍。唉，当他们用手指拼写时，我发现有时很难理解他们的意思。总的来说，如果不能教会他们发音方法，那么采用手语字母似乎是最好、最便捷的交流方式。无论如何，我觉得不管使用什么设备，盲聋人都不可能学会使用手势。

  前几天，我遇见了一位失聪的挪威绅士，他很熟悉瑞根希德·卡塔和她的老师。我们说起了卡塔，进行了愉快的交谈。他说卡塔勤勉而快乐。她会纺纱，还钩了许多编织品。她阅读书籍，过着愉快而有意义的生活。

可想不到的是，她竟然不会用手语字母！她很会读唇，如果她弄不懂某个短语，她的朋友就帮她写在手上，她就用这种方法与陌生人交谈。但我却不能完全辨认出别人写在我手上的所有东西，所以您看，在某些方面瑞根希德走在了我前面。我真希望有朝一日能见到她……

To Mr. William Wade

(*Wrentham, Mass., June 5, 1899.*)

…Linnie Haguewood's letter, which you sent me some weeks ago, interested me very much. It seemed to show spontaneity and great sweetness of character. I was a good deal amused by what she said about history. I am sorry she does not enjoy it; but I too feel sometimes how dark, and mysterious and even fearful the history of old peoples, old religions and old forms of government really is.

Well, I must confess, I do not like the sign-language, and I do not think it would be of much use to the deaf-blind. I find it very difficult to follow the rapid motions made by the deaf-mutes, and besides, signs seem a great hindrance to them in acquiring the power of using language easily and freely. Why, I find it hard to understand them sometimes when they spell on their fingers. On the whole, if they cannot be taught articulation, the manual alphabet seems the best and most convenient means of communication. At any rate, I am sure the deaf-blind cannot learn to use signs with any degree of facility.

The other day, I met a deaf Norwegian gentleman, who knows Ragnhild Kaata and her teacher very well, and we had a very interesting conversation about her. He said she was very industrious and happy. She spins, and does a great deal of fancy work, and reads, and leads a pleasant, useful life. Just think, she cannot use the manual alphabet! She reads the lips well, and if she cannot understand a phrase, her friends write it in her hand; and in this way she converses with strangers. I cannot make out anything written in my hand, so you see, Ragnhild has got ahead of me in some things. I do hope I shall see her sometime…

海伦通过了拉德克利夫学院的入学考试，收到了学院的入学通知书，前后虽有波折，但她终于有机会成为一名大学生了。

致塞缪尔·理查德·富勒夫人

（伦瑟姆，1899年10月20日）

……我想现在是告诉您一些关于我们冬季计划的时候了。您知道，长期以来，我的志向一直就是要像许多别的女孩子那样，上拉德克利夫学院，获得学位；但目前，拉德克利夫的欧文院长却劝说我走一条特别的道路。她说，我能克服许多障碍而顺利通过所有考试，这已向世界证明我可以适应大学的功课。她向我表明，对我而言，更好的追求是发掘培养自己的写作能力，而不是仅仅为了要像其他女孩子一样，就在拉德克利夫学习四年的课程，这其实是非常愚蠢的一件事。她还说，她不认为一纸学位有什么真正价值，并且觉得根据实际情况做出选择要比仅仅为了学位而去浪费精力更可取。她的观点似乎是明智可行的，我不得不接受它。但我发现，要放弃上大学的念头是非常非常困难的；当我还是个小女孩时，这个念头就已在我脑子里生根了。但仅仅因为某人长期以来一直想做某件事，就不管这事是否愚蠢或无用，而非要坚持去做，这也不对吧？

但是，当我们讨论冬季计划时，黑尔博士很久前的一个建议闪现在老师的脑海——我可以在相关科任教授的指导下，学习一些类似拉德克利夫学院设置的课程。欧文小姐似乎也不反对这个提议，并友好地去拜访这些教授，以了解他们是否愿意给我上课。如果有热心教授愿意教我，如果我们有足够的钱去履行我们的计划，那么我今年学习的将会是英语、伊丽莎白时期的英国文学、拉丁语和德语……

To Mrs. Samuel Richard Fuller

(*Wrentham, October 20, 1899.*)

…I suppose it is time for me to tell you something about our plans for the winter. You know it has long been my ambition to go to Radcliffe, and receive a degree, as many other girls have done, but Dean Irwin of Radcliffe, has persuaded me to take a special course for the present. She said I had already shown the world that I could do the college work, by passing all my examinations successfully, in spite of many obstacles. She showed me how very foolish it would be for me to pursue a four years' course of study at Radcliffe, simply to be like other girls, when I might better be cultivating whatever ability I had for writing. She said she did not consider a degree of any real value, but thought it was much more desirable to do something original than to waste one's energies only for a degree. Her arguments seemed so wise and practical, that I could not but yield. I found it hard, very hard, to give up the idea of going to college; it had been in my mind ever since I was a little girl; but there is no use doing a foolish thing, because one has wanted to do it a long time, is there?

But, while we were discussing plans for the winter, a suggestion which Dr. Hale had made long ago flashed across Teacher's mind—that I might take courses somewhat like those offered at Radcliffe, under the instruction of the professors in those courses. Miss Irwin seemed to have no objection to this proposal, and kindly offered to see the professors and find out if they would give me lessons. If they will be so good as to teach me and if we have money enough to do as we have planned, my studies this year will be English, English Literature of the Elizabethan period, Latin and German…

致约翰·希茨先生

（剑桥布莱特街138号，1899年11月11日）

……说到盲文问题，当我听说自己关于考试的看法被他人质疑时，我真是伤心极了。这些质疑和矛盾的根源似乎就是无知。哎呀！连您自己好像都认为我教你的是美式盲文，其实您对该系统连一个字母都不认识！当您说自己在用美式盲文给我写信时——其实您用的是英式盲文，一想到这事，我就会不由自主地笑起来！

以下是用盲文考试的情况说明：

我如何通过拉德克利夫学院的入学考试

1899年6月29日至30日，我参加了拉德克利夫学院的入学考试。第一天考初级希腊语和高级拉丁语，第二天考几何、代数和高级希腊语。

学院管理层不允许沙利文小姐为我读试卷，所以，学校就聘请帕金斯盲人学院教师尤金·C.维宁先生，用盲文为我抄写试卷。维宁先生对我而言完全是个陌生人，除了通过用盲文书写，我跟他是无法交流的。此外，监考人也是位陌生人，他也不打算同我做任何交流。由于他们两人对我发音的方式并不熟悉，所以根本听不懂我跟他们说的话。

不管怎样，盲文足以胜任语言表达；但如果要用盲文表示几何和代数，那就困难重重了。尤其是代数，我在这科上浪费了许多宝贵时间，仍是稀里糊涂，这真使我感到灰心丧气。事实上，我对自己国家通用的所有表达文字的盲文都很熟悉——英式、美式，以及纽约点式；但这三种系统中，对几何和代数的各种符号及标记的表示方法是截然不同的，而在考试前两天，我在数学上还只使用过英式盲文。我的整个学习过程中用的都是英式，从未用过其他系统。

在几何考试中，我遇到的主要问题是：过去我一直习惯于阅读一行行印制的命题，或是让人把命题拼写在我手上；但考试时最莫名其妙地的是，虽然命题就在我面前，我还是对那些盲文一头雾水，无法把读到的内容清晰地在大脑里组合出来。在考代数时，我感到更加艰难——那些一知半解的符号成了我的"拦路虎"。本来我刚刚学过那些符号，以为已弄懂它们了，但考试时碰到却仍然令我茫然不知所措。因此，我答题时缓慢而费力，不得不反复阅读答题示例，才能勉强搞清答题要求。其实，直到现在我也不敢说我能正确读懂所有的符号。特别是当我心灰意冷之时，我觉得很难让自己保持头脑清醒……

有关吉尔曼先生写给您的信，现在我想澄清一个事实。在吉尔曼的学校，我从未接受过任何直接指导。沙利文小姐总是坐在我旁边，把老师说的话告诉我。我确实教过我的物理老师霍尔小姐如何书写美式盲文，但她并未用美式盲文给我做过什么指导。当然，她曾用盲文书写过几道习题，但却浪费了我许多宝贵时间去辨认它们，也许这也可称之为"指导"吧。敬爱的弗兰·格罗特学过手语字母，她常常亲自教我，但这纯属私下补课，费用由我的朋友们帮我支付。而在德语课堂上，都是由沙利文小姐尽其所能，帮我翻译老师的授课内容。

如果您能把这封信的复印件寄给剑桥学校的校长，也许会有助于启发他弄清一些事实，以前他似乎对此全然不知……

To Mr. John Hitz

(*138 Brattle St. , Cambridge, Nov. 11, 1899.*)

…As to the braille question, I cannot tell how deeply it distresses me to hear that my statement with regard to the examinations has been doubted. Ignorance seems to be at the bottom of all those contradictions. Why, you yourself seem to think that I taught you American braille, when you do not know a single letter in the system! I could not help laughing when you said you had been writing to me in American braille—and there you were writing your letter in English braille!

The facts about the braille examinations are as follows:

How I passed my Entrance Examinations for Radcliffe College.

On the 29th and 30th of June, 1899, I took my examinations for Radcliffe College. The first day I had elementary Greek and advanced Latin, and the second day Geometry, Algebra and advanced Greek.

The college authorities would not permit Miss Sullivan to read the examination papers to me; so Mr. Eugene C. Vining, one of the instructors at the Perkins Institution for the Blind, was employed to copy the papers for me in braille. Mr. Vining was a perfect stranger to me, and could not communicate with me except by writing in braille. The Proctor also was a stranger, and did not attempt to communicate with me in any way; and, as they were both unfamiliar with my speech, they could not readily understand what I said to them.

However, the braille worked well enough in the languages; but when it came to Geometry and Algebra, it was quite different. I was sorely perplexed, and felt quite discouraged, and wasted much precious time, especially in Algebra. It is true that I am perfectly familiar with all literary braille—English, American and New York Point; but the method of writing the various signs used in Geometry and Algebra in the three systems is very different, and two days before the examinations I knew only the English method. I had used it, all through my school work, and never any other system.

In Geometry, my chief difficulty was, that I had always been accustomed to reading the propositions in Line Print, or having them spelled into my hand; and somehow, although the propositions were right before me, yet the braille confused me, and I could not fix in my mind clearly what I was reading. But, when I took up Algebra. I had a harder time still—I was terribly handicapped by my imperfect knowledge of the notation. The signs, which I had learned the day before, and which I thought I knew perfectly, confused me. Consequently my work was painfully slow, and I was obliged to read the examples over and over before I could form a clear idea what I was required to do. Indeed, I am not sure now that I read all the signs correctly, especially as I was much distressed, and found it very hard to keep my wits about me…

Now there is one more fact, which I wish to state very plainly, in regard to what Mr. Gilman wrote to you. I never received any direct instruction in the Gilman School. Miss Sullivan always sat beside me, and told me what the teachers said. I did teach Miss Hall, my teacher in Physics, how to write the American braille, but she never gave me any instruction by means of it, unless a few problems written for practice, which made me waste much precious time deciphering them, can be called instruction. Dear Frau Grote learned the manual alphabet, and used to teach me herself; but this was in private lessons, which were paid for by my friends. In the German class Miss Sullivan interpreted to me as well as she could what the teacher said.

Perhaps, if you would send a copy of this to the head of the Cambridge School, it might enlighten his mind on a few subjects, on which he seems to be in total darkness just now…

致米尔德丽德·凯勒小姐

（剑桥布莱特街138号，1899年11月26日）

……最终，我们在冬季安定下来，一切进展顺利。基思先生每天下午四点钟过来给我上课，使我在那条每个学生必经的崎岖道路上，取得"不断的进步"。我正在学习英国历史、英国文学、法语和拉丁语。不久以后，我还要学习德语和英语写作——让我们一起"哀号"吧！你知道，我和你一样讨厌语法，但如果要写作，就必须学好它。如同我们在学会游泳前，不得不上百次潜入湖中进行练习！在法语方面，老师正在给我读《科伦巴》，这是一部引人入胜的小说，充满了活泼有趣的措辞和令人毛骨悚然的冒险（你可别怪我用这些夸张的词汇呀，你不是也这么做嘛！）。如果你曾读过这本书，我想你会立刻喜欢上它的。你是不是正在学习英国历史？哇，这可是非常有趣的！我正在透彻地学习伊丽莎白时期的历史——宗教改革、确立英皇权力高于教会的《至尊法案》和《尊奉英国国教法令》，以及海上发现和其他一些大事，这些"见鬼的东西"似乎是专门被发明出来，用来折磨像你这样天真无邪的小孩子的！……

现在，我们已穿上臃肿的冬季全套装备——上衣、帽子、长外衣和法兰绒衣服等。我们刚刚请一位法国裁缝做了四套漂亮的礼服。有两套是我的，其中一套包括镶着黑色蕾丝花边的黑丝裙、配有天蓝色丝绒和雪纺绸的白府绸背心，以及镶着奶油色蕾丝花边的缎子上衣披肩。另一套是羊毛的，是非常清爽的绿色；其背心装饰着粉红和绿色的织锦丝绒，还有白色的蕾丝；胸前是双排扣，装饰着丝绒打成的褶子，还有一排小巧的白纽扣。老师也有一套丝质礼服，其裙子是黑的，背心大部分是黄色的，装饰着精美的淡紫色雪纺绸，以及黑丝绒蝴蝶结和花边。老师的另一套礼服是紫色的，装饰着紫色的丝绒，背心的领子上有奶油色的花边。所以，你可以想象一下，我们穿上礼服后，看起来多么像孔雀呀！只是我们没有尾巴而已……

八天前，哈佛和耶鲁两所大学之间举行了一场精彩的足球赛，现场气氛很热烈。我们在房间里就能清楚听到男生的叫喊声和观众的欢呼声，仿佛身临其境在现场观看一样。罗斯福上校也参加了比赛，他是哈佛队的；上帝保佑，他穿的竟是一件白色球衣，而不是我们所熟知的深红色！现场大约有两万五千人，当我们赶到那里时，处处人声鼎沸，我们也欣喜若狂。我们还从未见识过这样的足球赛，这简直就像是喧嚣的战场。当然，尽管双方都奋力拼搏，但都未进球，于是我们大笑着说："哇！好啦，现在烧锅可不能笑茶壶黑了！"……

To Miss Mildred Keller

(*138 Brattle Street, Cambridge, November 26, 1899*)

…At last we are settled for the winter, and our work is going smoothly. Mr. Keith comes every afternoon at four o'clock, and gives me a "friendly lift" over the rough stretches of road, over which every student must go. I am studying English history, English literature, French and Latin, and by and by I shall take up German and English composition—let us groan! You know, I detest grammar as much as you do; but I suppose I must go through it if I am to write, just as we had to get ducked in the lake hundreds of times before we could swim! In French Teacher is reading "Columba" to me. It is a delightful novel, full of piquant expressions and thrilling adventures (don't dare to blame me for using big words, since you do the same!) and, if you ever read it, I think you will enjoy it immensely. You are studying English history, aren't you? O but it's exceedingly interesting! I'm making quite a thorough study of the Elizabethan period—of the Reformation, and the Acts of Supremacy and Conformity, and the maritime discoveries, and all the big things, which the "deuce" seems to have invented to plague innocent youngsters like yourself!…

Now we have a swell winter outfit—coats, hats, gowns, flannels and all. We've just had four lovely dresses made by a French dressmaker. I have two, of which one has a black silk skirt, with a black lace net over it, and a waist of white poplin, with turquoise velvet and chiffon, and cream lace over a satin yoke. The other is woollen, and of a very pretty green. The waist is trimmed with pink and green brocaded velvet, and white lace, I think, and has double reefers on the front, tucked and trimmed with velvet, and also a row of tiny white buttons. Teacher too has a silk dress. The skirt is black, while the waist is mostly yellow, trimmed with delicate lavender chiffon, and black velvet bows and lace. Her other dress is purple, trimmed with purple velvet, and the waist has a collar of cream lace. So you may imagine that we look quite like peacocks, only we've no trains…

A week ago yesterday there was [a] great football game between Harvard and Yale, and there was tremendous excitement here. We could hear the yells of the boys and the cheers of the lookers-on as plainly in our room as if we had been on the field. Colonel Roosevelt was there, on Harvard's side; but bless you, he wore a white sweater, and no crimson that we know of ! There were about twenty-five thousand people at the game, and when we went out, the noise was so terrific, we nearly jumped out of our skins, thinking it was the din of war, and not a football game that we heard. But, in spite of all their wild efforts, neither side was scored, and we all laughed and said, "Oh, well, now the pot can't call the kettle black!"…

致约翰·希茨先生

（剑桥布莱特街138号，1900年2月3日）

……我的学习比以前更有趣了。在拉丁语方面，我正在阅读贺拉斯的颂诗。虽然我发现很难翻译它们，但我仍觉得它们是我所读过的或将要读的拉丁语诗歌中最优美的篇章。在法语方面，我已读完《科伦巴》，正在读高乃依⑮的《贺拉斯》⑯和拉·封丹⑰的《寓言诗》，这两本书都是盲文版。两本书我都没读多少，但我知道自己应该会喜欢那些寓言的，因为它们写得引人入胜，用简朴有趣的方式告诉了人们深刻的哲理。我好像没跟您提过我亲爱的老师正在给我读《仙后》⑱一书，恐怕我对这部诗作的评价只能是毁誉参半。我不太喜欢隐含象征意义的作品，事实上，我常常觉得这类作品很无聊。我不由自主地觉得斯宾塞的那个满是骑士、异教徒、仙女、龙和各种怪物的世界多少有些荒诞不经和滑稽可笑；但其诗句写得很优美，音韵悦耳，宛如一条叮咚流淌的小溪。

我现在已是15本新书的骄傲主人了，这些书是从路易斯维尔市订购的。它们之中包括《亨利·埃斯蒙德》⑲《培根散文集》⑳和《英国文学集萃》。也许下周我还会收到更多的新书，如《暴风雨》㉑和《仲夏夜之梦》㉒，或许还有格林的《英国历史选集》。您看，我是不是很有福气呀？

⑮高乃依（1606—1684）是17世纪法国古典主义悲剧的代表作家，被称为法国古典主义戏剧的奠基人。
⑯贺拉斯（公元前65年—公元前8年），古罗马诗人、批评家。其美学思想见于写给皮索父子的诗体长信《诗艺》。
⑰拉·封丹（1621—1695），法国寓言诗人。其代表作《寓言诗》是世界上最早的诗体寓言集。
⑱《仙后》是英国诗人埃德曼·斯宾塞（1552—1599）于1590年出版的史诗。诗人在《仙后》中创造的诗体被称为"斯宾塞诗节"。
⑲《亨利·埃斯蒙德》是英国维多利亚时代的小说家威廉·梅克比斯·萨克雷（1811—1863）的作品。
⑳弗朗西斯·培根，英国文艺复兴时期的散文家、哲学家，思想成熟，言论深邃，富含哲理。
㉑《暴风雨》是莎士比亚的最后一部作品。
㉒《仲夏夜之梦》是莎士比亚最富幻想色彩和浪漫情调的喜剧。

也许我的这封信对书籍讲得太多了——但是，这些天来，书籍确实占据了我的整个生活，因为我几乎不能看到或听到其他任何事物！我真的是每晚都枕着书籍入梦！您要知道，学生的生活范围多少有些狭窄，也有很多局限性；除了书籍，其他的一切基本都被排除在外……

To Mr. John Hitz

(*138 Brattle Street, Cambridge, Feb. 3, 1900.*)

…My studies are more interesting than ever. In Latin, I am reading Horace's odes. Although I find them difficult to translate, yet I think they are the loveliest pieces of Latin poetry I have read or shall ever read. In French we have finished "Colomba," and I am reading "Horace" by Corneille and La Fontaine's fables, both of which are in braille. I have not gone far in either; but I know I shall enjoy the fables, they are so delightfully written, and give such good lessons in a simple and yet attractive way. I do not think I have told you that my dear teacher is reading "The Faery Queen" to me. I am afraid I find fault with the poem as much as I enjoy it. I do not care much for the allegories, indeed I often find them tiresome, and I cannot help thinking that Spenser's world of knights, paynims, fairies, dragons and all sorts of strange creatures is a somewhat grotesque and amusing world; but the poem itself is lovely and as musical as a running brook.

I am now the proud owner of about fifteen new books, which we ordered from Louisville. Among them are "Henry Esmond, " "Bacon's Essays" and extracts from "English Literature." Perhaps next week I shall have some more books. "The Tempest," "A Midsummer Night's Dream" and possibly some selections from Green's history of England. Am I not very fortunate?

I am afraid this letter savors too much of books—but really they make up my whole life these days, and I scarcely see or hear of anything else! I do believe I sleep on books every night! You know a student's life is of necessity somewhat circumscribed and narrow and crowds out almost everything that is not in books...

致拉德克利夫学院学术委员会主席

（马萨诸塞州剑桥布莱特街138号，1900年5月5日）

尊敬的先生：

为了有助于我制订明年的学习计划，我谨向您提出申请，请您提供我能否在拉德克利夫学院选修正式课程的相关信息。

自从去年7月收到拉德克利夫学院给我的录取通知书以后，我一直在接受一位私人教师的辅导，已学习了贺拉斯、埃斯库罗斯、法语、德语、修辞学、英国历史、英国文学和评论，以及英语写作等。

在拉德克利夫学院，如果不能继续学习上述所有的课程，那么我希望至少能够学习其中的大部分课程。在我学习的过程中，需要沙利文小姐的陪伴。13年来，她一直是我的老师和伙伴，她翻译我说的话，并为我读试卷。在学院的课堂里或在背诵时，她必须和我在一起；当然，在某些科目中也可能是其他人来陪我。我所有的书面作业都只能用打字机来完成。如果教授听不懂我的话，我可以把问题的答案写出来，背诵完答案后再交给他。

不知贵院能否考虑上述这些前所未有的情况，做一些适当调整，以使我能够在拉德克利夫追求我的学业？我知道自己在接受大学教育的道路上困难重重——在别人看来，这或许是无法逾越的鸿沟；但是亲爱的先生，一名真正的士兵在战役开始之前是不会承认失败的。

To The Chairman of the Academic Board of Radcliffe College

(138 Brattle Street, Cambridge, Mass., May 5, 1900.)

Dear Sir:

As an aid to me in determining my plans for study the coming year, I apply to you for information as to the possibility of my taking the regular courses in Radcliffe College.

Since receiving my certificate of admission to Radcliffe last July, I have been studying with a private tutor, Horace, Aeschylus, French, German, Rhetoric, English History, English Literature and Criticism, and English composition.

In college I should wish to continue most, if not all of these subjects. The conditions under which I work require the presence of Miss Sullivan, who has been my teacher and companion for thirteen years, as an interpreter of oral speech and as a reader of examination papers. In college she, or possibly in some subjects some one else, would of necessity be with me in the lecture-room and at recitations. I should do all my written work on a typewriter, and if a Professor could not understand my speech, I could write out my answers to his questions and hand them to him after the recitation.

Is it possible for the College to accommodate itself to these unprecedented conditions, so as to enable me to pursue my studies at Radcliffe? I realize that the obstacles in the way of my receiving a college education are very great—to others they may seem insurmountable; but, dear Sir, a tree soldier does not acknowledge defeat before the battle.

这年秋天，凯勒进入了拉德克利夫学院，如愿以偿地成为一名正式大学生。

致约翰·希茨先生

（剑桥柯立芝大道14号，1900年11月26日）

……有关她和我计划为盲聋儿童建一所学校的事，已经与您交流过了。起初，我热情洋溢地支持这件事，但我做梦也想不到，除了那些对老师怀有敌意的人之外，还会有其他人极力反对这事；但是现在，经过认真思考并和我朋友商量之后，我做出了决定，这个计划绝对不可行。我因渴望其他盲聋儿童能像我一样拥有良好的学习条件，而几乎忘了要想实现这样的计划，期间必定会遇到许多困难。

我的朋友们认为我们可以在自己家里收一两个学生，这样既可以保证我对他们提供帮助，又避免了建一所大学校所面临的不利因素。他们都很善良；但我仍觉得他们更多的是从做生意的角度而不是从人道主义的角度来看问题。我确信他们并不十分了解我，我热切期盼所有像我一样遭受不幸的人，都能够有机会接受合适的教育，继承思想、知识和爱的遗产。当然，对于别人的看法所产生的压力，我也不能置之不理。我清楚地知道我必须放弃这个不切实际的计划。朋友们还说，我在拉德克利夫学院期间，应该委托一个顾问委员会来管理自己的事务。我仔细考虑了这个建议，然后对罗德斯先生说，当面临一些重大事项时，如果我能有一批睿智的朋友可以征询意见，那么我将感到自豪和高兴。我选择六个人组成这个委员会：我的母亲、老师（因为对我来说，她就像母亲一样）、胡顿夫人、罗德斯先生、格瑞尔博士和罗杰斯先生。这些年来，他们一直支持着我，使我得以进入大学。胡顿夫人已经写信给我母亲，表示如果我母亲答应除了母亲本人和老师之外，还愿意再给我找几名顾问，那么可以给她发电报。今天早上我们收到了回函，母亲已同意这一安排。现在，我要做的就是给格瑞尔博士和罗杰斯先生写信……

我们和贝尔博士进行了一次长谈。最后他提了一个建议,让我们欣喜得无以言表。他说,试图为盲聋儿童建一所学校是一个非常盲目的计划,因为这样一来,这些孩子就会丧失进入正规学校的宝贵机会,不能与那些能听能看的孩子们一起融入丰富多彩的自由生活。当然,我对他的这种看法心存疑虑,但我也想不出该怎么做才能有助于解决这一问题。不管怎样,贝尔先生建议,对建学校计划感兴趣的朋友们可以成立一个促进盲聋儿童教育的协会,我和老师当然应加入其中。按照他的计划,协会要委派我老师去培训其他老师,由这些老师在盲聋儿童的家里对他们进行教育,就像我老师当年教我那样。筹集到的基金将用于支付教师们的食宿费和薪水。同时,贝尔博士还补充说,当我心中的伟大愿望付诸实施时,我就可以安心地在拉德克利夫和那些能看能听的姑娘们一起奋斗了。于是大家都鼓掌欢呼,接着——笑容满面地离去。现在,我和老师的心情是这段时间里从未有过的轻松。当然,目前我们还做不了什么,但我们已不再为我的大学学业和盲聋人的未来福利而痛苦焦虑了。请告诉我您对贝尔博士的建议有什么看法。我觉得这个建议似乎更可行也更明智些;但在我就此事发言或行动之前,我必须先将方方面面的情况都搞清楚才行……

To Mr. John Hitz

(*14 Coolidge Ave. Cambridge, Nov. 26, 1900.*)

…—has already communicated with you in regard to her and my plan of establishing an institution for deaf and blind children. At first I was most enthusiastic in its support, and I never dreamed that any grave objections could be raised except indeed by those who are hostile to Teacher; but now, after thinking most *seriously* and consulting my friends, I have decided that——'s plan is by no means feasible. In my eagerness to make it possible for deaf and blind children to have the same advantages that I have had, I quite forgot that there might be many obstacles in the way of my accomplishing anything like what——proposed.

My friends thought we might have one or two pupils in our own home, thereby securing to me the advantage of being helpful to others without any of the disadvantages of a large school. They were very kind; but I could not help feeling that they spoke more from a business than a humanitarian point of view. I am sure they did not quite understand how passionately I desire that all who are afflicted like myself shall receive their rightful inheritance of thought, knowledge and love. Still I could not shut my eyes to the force and weight of their arguments, and I saw plainly that I must abandon——'s scheme as impracticable. They also said that I ought to appoint an advisory committee to control my affairs while I am at Radcliffe. I considered this suggestion carefully, then I told Mr. Rhoades that I should be proud and glad to have wise friends to whom I could always turn for advice in all important matters. For this committee I chose six, my mother, Teacher, because she is like a mother to me, Mrs. Hutton, Mr. Rhoades, Dr. Greer and Mr. Rogers, because it is they who have supported me all these years and made it possible for me to enter college. Mrs. Hutton had already written to mother, asking her to telegraph if she was willing for me to have other advisers besides herself and Teacher. This morning we received word that mother had given her consent to this arrangement. Now it remains for me to write to Dr. Greer and Mr. Rogers…

We had a long talk with Dr. Bell. Finally he proposed a plan which delighted us all beyond words. He said that it was a gigantic blunder to attempt to found a school for deaf and blind children, because then they would lose the most precious opportunities of entering into the fuller, richer, freer life of seeing and hearing children. I had had misgivings on this point; but I could not see how we were to help it. However Mr. Bell suggested that——and all her friends who are interested in her scheme should organize an association for the promotion of the education of the deaf and blind, Teacher and myself being included, of course. Under his plan they were to appoint Teacher to train others to instruct deaf and blind children in their own homes, just as she had taught me. Funds were to be raised for the teachers' lodgings and also for their salaries. At the same time Dr. Bell added that I could rest content and fight my way through Radcliffe in competition with seeing and hearing girls, while the great desire of my heart was being fulfilled. We clapped our hands and shouted;—went away beaming with pleasure, and Teacher and I felt more light of heart than we had for sometime. Of course we can do nothing just now; but the painful anxiety about my college work and the future welfare of the deaf and blind has been lifted from our minds. Do tell me what you think about Dr. Bell's suggestion. It seems most practical and wise to me; but I must know all that there is to be known about it before I speak or act in the matter…

致约翰·D. 莱特先生

（剑桥，1900年12月9日）

难道您认为我是一个小顽童吗？我简直想不出一个足够恶劣的词来表达您对我的看法，也许"盗马贼"一词能符合您的心意吧。请跟我说实话，您认为我真有那么坏吗？我希望您不是这么看的。我曾计划给您写许多信，可都未付诸实施。但我很高兴能收到您的信，是的，我真的很高兴，并且我打算立即给您回信。无奈的是，当人们忙碌的时候，时光总是不经意地溜走，而今年秋天我一直忙得不可开交。请相信这是事实，拉德克利夫的姑娘们总是孜孜不倦地专注于学业。如果您对此有任何怀疑之处，那么请您最好亲自来看看。

是的，我为了获得学位而选修了常规课程。当我获得文学学士之时，我想您就不敢再叫我小顽童了吧！我正在学习英语——大二的英语（虽然我看不出大二的英语与普通英语有什么不同之处）。我还在学习德语、法语和历史，不知您对此是否满意？我非常努力地学习，比我自己所期望的还要勤勉，这也是我证明自己很愿意上大学的一种方式。有时的确很艰难，困难重重，但我从未被困难吓倒。不，我没有学习数学、希腊语或拉丁语。拉德克利夫的课程是可以选修的，只有某些英语方面的课程是必修课。由于我在入学前就已通过了英语和高级法语考试，所以我选修的都是我最喜欢的课程。但我并不打算全部放弃拉丁语和希腊语，或许我以后将选修这些科目。可是，我要永远跟数学说再见了。我向您保证，我是多么愿意乐滋滋地最后再看一眼这些可怕的妖精们啊！我希望经过四年的学习，我能拿到学位，但我也不是非常看重学位。没必要匆匆忙忙的，我还想多涉猎一些学习之外的东西。如果我一年只学两门功课，甚或是一门功课，我的许多朋友也会很高兴的，但我非常反感在学院里度过自己的业余生活……

To Mr. John D. Wright

(*Cambridge, December 9, 1900.*)

Do you think me a villain and—I can't think of a word bad enough to express your opinion of me, unless indeed horse-thief will answer the purpose. Tell me truly, do you think me as bad as that? I hope not; for I have thought many letters to you which never got on paper, and I am delighted to get your good letter, yes, I really was, and I intended to answer it immediately; but the days slip by unnoticed when one is busy, and I have been very busy this fall. You must believe that. Radcliffe girls are always up to their ears in work. If you doubt it, you'd better come and see for yourself.

Yes, I am taking the regular college course for a degree. When I am a

B. A., I suppose you will not dare call me a villain! I am studying English—Sophomore English, if you please, (though I can't see that it is different from just plain English) German, French and History. I'm enjoying my work even more than I expected to, which is another way of saying that I'm glad I came. It is hard, very hard at times; but it hasn't swamped me yet. No, I am not studying Mathematics, or Greek or Latin either. The courses at Radcliffe are elective, only certain courses in English are prescribed. I passed off my English and advanced French before I entered college, and I choose the courses I like best. I don't however intend to give up Latin and Greek entirely. Perhaps I shall take up these studies later; but I've said goodbye to Mathematics forever, and I assure you, I was delighted to see the last of those horrid goblins! I hope to obtain my degree in four years; but I'm not very particular about that. There's no great hurry, and I want to get as much as possible out of my studies. Many of my friends would be well pleased if I would take two or even one course a year; but I rather object to spending the rest of my life in college…

致威廉·韦德先生

（剑桥柯立芝大道14号，1900年12月9日）

……既然您这么关注盲聋人，那么我要告诉您近来我听说的几件事。去年10月，我听说在德克萨斯州有一个非常聪明的小女孩，她的名字叫鲁比·赖斯，大约13岁。她从未受过教育，但人们说她会做针线活，还喜欢帮助别人做这类活计。她的嗅觉很灵敏。哎呀，当她走进一家商店时，能径直走到玻璃陈列柜前；她还能分辨出哪些是她自己的东西。她的父母非常焦急地想为她找一位老师。他们还给希茨先生写信介绍了她的情况。

我还知道在密西西比州聋人学校的一个孩子，她的名字叫莫德·斯考特，年方6岁。负责照料她的沃金斯小姐给我写了一封非常感人的信。沃金斯小姐说莫德生来就失聪，只有3个月大时又不幸失明。在她来到聋人学校之前的那几个星期，她完全无依无靠。她不会走路，甚至也不太会用双手做事。当老师们试图教她用线穿珠子时，她的一双小手只会垂在身旁。显然，她的触觉发育不良。到现在为止，她只有抓住别人的手才能行走。但她似乎是个很聪明的孩子。沃金斯小姐还补充说她非常美丽。我在给沃金斯小姐的回信中说：在莫德学会阅读之后，我要寄很多故事书给她。每当我想到这个甜美可爱的小姑娘完全被隔绝在生活中所有的美好事物之外时，我就感到心痛不已。不过沃金斯小姐也许正是她所需要的那种老师。

不久前，我在纽约遇见了罗德斯小姐，她告诉我她曾见到过凯提·麦克吉尔。她说，这个可怜的少女说话和做事时完全像个小孩子。当时，凯提玩着罗德斯小姐的戒指，她把戒指拿走，然后欢快地笑着说："您再也找不着它们啦！"只有当罗德斯小姐讲一些最简单的事情时，她才能听得懂。罗德斯小姐想送给她一些书，但却找不到浅显得能适合她读的书！她说凯提的确很可爱，但令人遗憾的是，她缺乏合适的教导。我听到这些后感到很震惊，因为从您的来信中，我曾判定凯提是个非常早熟的女孩……

几天前，我在伦瑟姆火车站遇见了汤米·斯特林格。他现在是位高大而健壮的男生了，很快，就需要一位男士来照顾他了。因为他的确太高了，女士很难照顾好他的。我听说他上了公立学校，并取得了惊人的进步。但到目前为止，他的谈吐却没表现出这些，他在谈话中仅会说"是"和"不是"……

To Mr. William Wade

（*14 Coolidge Avenue, Cambridge, December 9, 1900*）

…Since you are so much interested in the deaf and blind, I will begin by telling you of several cases I have come across lately. Last October I heard of an unusually bright little girl in Texas. Her name is Ruby Rice, and she is thirteen years old, I think. She has never been taught; but they say she can sew and likes to help others in this sort of work. Her sense of smell is wonderful. Why, when she enters a store, she will go straight to the showcases, and she can also distinguish her own things. Her parents are very anxious indeed to find a teacher for her. They have also written to Mr. Hitz about her.

I also know a child at the Institution for the Deaf in Mississippi. Her name is Maud Scott, and she is six years old. Miss Watkins, the lady who has charge of her wrote me a most interesting letter. She said that Maud was born deaf and lost her sight when she was only three months old, and that when she went to the Institution a few weeks ago, she was quite helpless. She could not even walk and had very little use of her hands. When they tried to teach her to string beads, her little hands fell to her side. Evidently her sense of touch has not been developed, and as yet she can walk only when she holds some one's hand; but she seems to be an exceedingly bright child. Miss Watkins adds that she is very pretty. I have written to her that when Maud learns to read. I shall have many stories to send her. The dear, sweet little girl, it makes my heart ache to think how utterly she is cut off from all that is good and desirable in life. But Miss Watkins seems to be just the kind of teacher she needs.

I was in New York not long ago and I saw Miss Rhoades, who told me that she had seen Katie McGirr. She said the poor young girl talked and acted exactly like a little child. Katie played with Miss Rhoades's rings and took them away, saying with a merry laugh, "You shall not have them again!" She could only understand Miss Rhoades when she talked about the simplest things. The latter wished to send her some books; but she could not find anything simple enough for her! She said Katie was very sweet indeed, but sadly in need of proper instruction. I was much surprised to hear all this; for I judged from your letters that Katie was a very precocious girl…

A few days ago I met Tommy Stringer in the railroad station at Wrentham. He is a great, strong boy now, and he will soon need a man to take care of him; he is really too big for a lady to manage. He goes to the public school, I hear, and his progress is astonishing, they say; but it doesn't show as yet in his conversation, which is limited to "Yes" and "No."…

致查尔斯·T.科普兰先生

（1900年12月20日）

尊敬的科普兰先生：

之所以冒昧地给您写这封信，是因为我担心如果不向您解释我停止写作文的原因，您就会以为我已丧失信心，或者想逃避批评，怯懦地从您的课堂上溜之大吉。请不要有上述这些不愉快的想法。事实上，我并未丧失信心，也不想逃避什么。我自信自己仍能像以前一样把作文写好，并且我相信自己可以在这门课上拿到高分。但我对这种"文学大杂烩"已失去兴趣。我对自己的表现从来就没有满意过，直到经过您的指点，我才明白自己的问题所在。10月份，当我迈进您的课堂时，我像其他同学一样尽心尽力，几乎忘了自己的缺陷和所处的特殊环境。但不管怎样，现在我终于明白了，如果某人想用不配套的马具把自己的马车拴在一颗星星上，那绝对是好高骛远，不切实际的。

我总是理所当然地接受别人通过观察得来的经验和意见。但我从来没有想过：应该通过观察来描写出自己独特的经历，这样的文章才有价值。从今以后，我下定决心要过自己的生活，写自己的所思所想。当我真正写出一些新颖、自然而优雅的东西，并觉得值得请您点评时，我就会把它送给您斧正。如果我写出了这样的文章，并且得到了您的肯定，那么我会很开心的；但如果您的评价是负面的，那么我也会坚持不懈地继续努力，直到成功写出令您满意的作品……

Mr. Charles T. Copeland

(*December 20, 1900.*)

My dear Mr. Copeland:

I venture to write to you because I am afraid that if I do not explain why I have stopped writing themes, you will think I have become discouraged, or perhaps that to escape criticism I have beat a cowardly retreat from your class. Please do not think either of these very unpleasant thoughts. I am not discouraged, nor am I afraid. I am confident that I could go on writing themes like those I have written, and I suppose I should get through the course with fairly good marks; but this sort of literary patchwork has lost all interest for me. I have never been satisfied with my work; but I never knew what my difficulty was until you pointed it out to me. When I came to your class last October, I was trying with all my might to be like everybody else, to forget as entirely as possible my limitations and peculiar environment. Now, however, I see the folly of attempting to hitch one's wagon to a star with harness that does not belong to it.

I have always accepted other people's experiences and observations as a matter of course. It never occurred to me that it might be worth while to make my own observations and describe the experiences peculiarly my own. Henceforth I am resolved to be myself, to live my own life and write my own thoughts when I have any. When I have written something that seems to be fresh and spontaneous and worthy of your criticisms, I will bring it to you, if I may, and if you think it good, I shall be happy; but if your verdict is unfavorable, I shall try again and yet again until I have succeeded in pleasing you…

九

多彩的生活还在继续

在以下这封信中，海伦回复了《圆圆大世界》编辑的临时提议，这位编辑建议，如果能有足够多的订阅者，那么该杂志可以为盲人们出版盲文版。盲人们应该拥有一本好的杂志，显然，《圆圆大世界》盲文版如果得以出版，它将是用压印浮凸字母印刷的最好的月刊之一。可是，单靠盲人订阅者是不可能支撑起这本杂志的，还需要许多经费来弥补那些额外的开支。

致《圆圆大世界》的编辑

（剑桥，1901年2月16日）

纽约市《圆圆大世界》编辑部

尊敬的先生：直到今天，我才抽出空来回复您那有趣的来信。已经有消息灵通的人士告诉了我这个好消息，但是能直接从你们那得到消息，仍令我倍感高兴。

如果能用"可被触摸的语言"来出版《圆圆大世界》，那真是棒极了。但我很怀疑那些拥有奇妙视力的人们能否理解你们的周密计划会对盲人们带来的益处。能够通过阅读来了解世人的愿望、思想和行为，以及令人感兴趣的欢喜、忧伤、失败和成功的故事——这的确是一种无法言说的幸福。我相信，《圆圆大世界》为了给坐在黑暗中的人们带去光明而付出的努力，必将会收到应有的鼓励和支持。

但我怀疑，订阅盲文版《圆圆大世界》的人也许不会太多，因为据我所知，盲人是一个贫穷的阶层。可是，如果有必要的话，为什么盲人的朋友们不能援助《圆圆大世界》呢？仁慈的人们肯定已准备好了，他们将伸出援手，献出爱心，让慷慨的意向转化成高尚的行为。

衷心祝愿你们事业有成！这项事业对于我来说是弥足珍贵的。

To *The Great Round World*

(*Cambridge, Feb. 16, 1901.*)

The Great Round World, *New York City.*

Gentlemen: I have only to-day found time to reply to your interesting letter. A little bird had already sung the good news in my ear; but it was doubly pleasant to have it straight from you.

It would be splendid to have *The Great Round World* printed in "language that can be felt." I doubt if any one who enjoys the wondrous privilege of seeing can have any conception of the boon such a publication as you contemplate would be to the sightless. To be able to read for one's self what is being willed, thought and done in the world—the world in whose joys and sorrows, failures and successes one feels the keenest interest—that would indeed be a happiness too deep for words. I trust that the effort of *The Great Round World* to bring light to those who sit in darkness will receive the encouragement and support it so richly deserves.

I doubt, however, if the number of subscribers to an embossed edition of *The Great Round World* would ever be large; for I am told that the blind as a class are poor. But why should not the friends of the blind assist *The Great Round World,* if necessary? Surely there are hearts and hands ever ready to make it possible for generous intentions to be wrought into noble deeds.

Wishing you godspeed in an undertaking that is very dear to my heart, I am, etc.

致尼娜·罗德斯小姐

（剑桥，1901年9月25日）

……我们在哈利法克斯一直待到了八月中旬……日复一日地参观港口、军舰和公园，我们忙碌地思考、感知和欣赏着这一切……当"印第安纳号"访问哈利法克斯时，我们乘坐从她上面放下的汽艇，应邀登船。我摩挲着巨大的加农炮，用手指读着在圣地亚哥捕获的几条西班牙船只的名字，也触摸了她那曾被炮弹击穿的地方。"印第安纳号"是港口里最威武雄壮的船，我们为她而感到骄傲。

当我们离开哈利法克斯之后，我们拜访了住在布雷顿角的贝尔博士。他有一幢建在贝恩·布瑞夫山上的房子，面朝着布拉斯德奥尔湖，造型别致，浪漫优雅……

贝尔博士给我讲了他的许多工作趣事。他刚刚造了一条船，可以用一只顺风飞翔的风筝来驱动。有一天，他做了一个试验，想看看在逆风情况下，风筝是否也可以牵引小船。当时我也在场帮他放风筝。我注意到有一只风筝的线是金属丝做的，凭着自己曾用线穿珠子的经验，我告诉贝尔博士说，这线可能会断。但贝尔博士却自信地说："不会的！"接着，他放飞了这只风筝。风筝开始费力地向前飞，拖曳着、挣扎着。哎呦！线突然断了，那只庞大的红龙栽了下来。贝尔博士绝望地站在那，盯着它。从那以后，贝尔博士总会问我风筝线牢不牢，如果我的回答是否定的，他就会立刻换掉这线。总之，我们在一起非常开心……

To Miss Nina Rhoades

(*Cambridge, Sept. 25, 1901.*)

…We remained in Halifax until about the middle of August…Day after day the Harbor, the warships, and the park kept us busy thinking and feeling and enjoying…When the *Indiana* visited Halifax, we were invited to go on board, and she sent her own launch for us. I touched the immense cannon, read with my fingers several of the names of the Spanish ships that were captured at Santiago, and felt the places where she had been pierced with shells. The *Indiana* was the largest and finest ship in the Harbor, and we felt very proud of her.

After we left Halifax, we visited Dr. Bell at Cape Breton. He has a charming, romantic house on a mountain called Beinn Bhreagh, which overlooks the Bras d'Or Lake…

Dr. Bell told me many interesting things about his work. He had just constructed a boat that could be propelled by a kite with the wind in its favor, and one day he tried experiments to see if he could steer the kite against the wind. I was there and really helped him fly the kites. On one of them I noticed that the strings were of wire, and having had some experience in bead work, I said I thought they would break. Dr. Bell said "No!" with great confidence, and the kite was sent up. It began to pull and tug, and lo, the wires broke, and off went the great red dragon, and poor Dr. Bell stood looking forlornly after it. After that he asked me if the strings were all right and changed them at once when I answered in the negative. Altogether we had great fun…

1901年11月11日，爱德华·埃弗里特·黑尔博士在波士顿翠蒙堂举行的"塞缪尔·格瑞德里·豪诞辰一百周年纪念会"上，朗读了以下这封信。

致爱德华·埃弗里特·黑尔博士

（剑桥，1901年11月10日）

老师和我期待出席将于明天举行的纪念豪博士一百周年诞辰的会议；但我很怀疑届时能否有机会与您说话。所以我现在就写信告诉您：得知您将要在会上发言，我非常高兴。因为我觉得在自己认识的所有人当中，只有您最适合代表那些得益于豪博士，才受了教育，拥有了机会和幸福的人们，去表达他们诚挚的感激之情。要感谢豪博士，是他开启了盲人的双眼，并让哑者学会了唇语。

现在，我坐在自己的书房里，周围环绕着我的书籍，我仿佛沉浸在伟人和智者亲切愉悦的陪伴之中。我极力设想，如果豪博士没有完成上帝赋予他的伟大使命，那么我的生活将会是怎样的呢？如果他没有亲自承担起教育劳拉·布里奇曼的重任，把她从地狱之洞领出来，回归人类传承的社会，那么我今天还会是拉德克利夫学院的二年级学生吗？谁能说得清这一切呢？但是，若要去假设这世上不曾有豪博士的伟大成就，那也是毫无意义的事。

我想，只有那些逃脱了生不如死的困境的人，比如劳拉·布里奇曼就是从这种困境中被拯救出来的，才能体会到如果一颗灵魂没有思想、没有信念或希望，那么它将是多么孤独啊！黑暗笼罩着它，它只能无可奈何地被禁锢着。语言是无法描述出那牢房的凄清，也无法描述出当那颗灵魂挣脱束缚后的欢欣的。如果我们比较一下豪博士开展工作之前盲人的无助和在其开展工作之后盲人的自立和贡献，那么我们就会意识到我们已取得了巨大的进步。假如身体缺陷令我们四周高墙林立，那该怎么办呢？要感谢我们的朋友和那些援助者们，是他们令我们的世界不断拓展，一直延伸到高远而辽阔的天堂！

令人欣慰的是，豪博士的高尚行为必将赢得世人的称颂、景仰和铭记。而波士顿这座城市，就是他为人类鞠躬尽瘁和取得辉煌胜利的地方。

借此机会，我和我的老师一起送上最诚挚的祝福。

您真诚的朋友

（海伦·凯勒）

To Dr. Edward Everett Hale

(*Cambridge, Nov. 10, 1901.*)

My teacher and I expect to be present at the meeting tomorrow in commemoration of the one hundredth anniversary of Dr. Howe's birth; but I very much doubt if we shall have an opportunity to speak with you; so I am writing now to tell you how delighted I am that you are to speak at the meeting, because I feel that you, better than any one I know will express the heartfelt gratitude of those who owe their education, their opportunities, their happiness to him who opened the eyes of the blind and gave the dumb lip language.

Sitting here in my study, surrounded by my books, enjoying the sweet and intimate companionship of the great and the wise, I am trying to realize what my life might have been, if Dr. Howe had failed in the great task God gave him to perform. If he had not taken upon himself the responsibility of Laura Bridgman's education and led her out of the pit of Acheron back to her human inheritance, should I be a sophomore at Radcliffe College today—who can say? But it is idle to speculate about what might have been in connection with Dr. Howe's great achievement.

I think only those who have escaped that death-in-life existence, from which Laura Bridgman was rescued, can realize how isolated, how shrouded in darkness, how cramped by its own impotence is a soul without thought or faith or hope. Words are powerless to describe the desolation of that prison-house, or the joy of the soul that is delivered out of its captivity. When we compare the needs and helplessness of the blind before Dr. Howe began his work, with their present usefulness and independence, we realize that great things have been done in our midst. What if physical conditions have built up high walls about us? Thanks to our friend and helper, our world lies upward; the length and breadth and sweep of the heavens are ours!

It is pleasant to think that Dr. Howe's noble deeds will receive their due tribute of affection and gratitude, in the city, which was the scene of his great labors and splendid victories for humanity.

With kind greetings, in which my teacher joins me, I am

Affectionately your friend,

HELEN KELLER.

致可敬的乔治·弗里斯比·霍尔先生

（马萨诸塞州剑桥，1901年11月25日）

尊敬的霍尔参议员：

我很高兴您喜欢我写的那封关于豪博士的信。那是我发自肺腑的真情实感，也许这就是为什么这封信能引起他人共鸣的原因吧。我要请黑尔博士把这封信借给我，这样，我就能抄写一份给您。

如您所知，我用着一台打字机，可以说——它是我的得力助手。如果没有它，我是不可能上大学的。我用它写作文，答考卷，甚至写希腊语。说实话，这台打字机只有一个缺点，或许在教授们看来这反倒是个优点，那就是只要匆匆扫一眼打字机打出的内容，就能发现错误之处；这样一来，我就不可能用潦草的字迹来掩饰错误了。

我知道当我告诉您我对政治很感兴趣时，您一定会忍俊不禁。说实

话，我喜欢请别人给我读报纸，并试着去理解当今社会的重大问题；但恐怕我的立场是不太坚定的，因为我每读一本新书，就会改变自己的观点。我曾以为，当我学习了公民政府和经济学后，我所有的难题和困惑都将迎刃而解，顺理成章地找到答案；可是，哎呀！我发现在知识的沃野里，莠草往往比麦子多得多……

To The Hon. George Frisbie Hoar

(*Cambridge, Mass., November 25, 1901*)

My Dear Senator Hoar:—

I am glad you liked my letter about Dr. Howe. It was written out of my heart, and perhaps that is why it met a sympathetic response in other hearts. I will ask Dr. Hale to lend me the letter, so that I can make a copy of it for you.

You see, I use a typewriter—it is my right hand man, so to speak. Without it I do not see how I could go to college. I write all my themes and examinations on it, even Greek. Indeed, it has only one drawback, and that probably is regarded as an advantage by the professors; it is that one's mistakes may be detected at a glance; for there is no chance to hide them in illegible writing.

I know you will be amused when I tell you that I am deeply interested in politics. I like to have the papers read to me, and I try to understand the great questions of the day; but I am afraid my knowledge is very unstable; for I change my opinions with every new book I read. I used to think that when I studied Civil Government and Economics, all my difficulties and perplexities would blossom into beautiful certainties; but alas, I find that there are more tares than wheat in these fertile fields of knowledge…

译后记

　　李月华编辑嘱咐我写篇译后记，我感谢她为出版此书付出的智慧和汗水。感谢江西人民出版社的支持，也感谢余晖老师一直以来对我的翻译工作所给予的指导和鼓励。

　　翻译本书的这半年多时光，是一次学习提高的历练，也是一段苦乐参半的日子。从小，海伦·凯勒就是我无比景仰的英雄，能有机会翻译她的作品，我甚感荣幸。于是，白天工作，夜深人静时，我就坐在电脑旁，噼啪敲打键盘，聚精会神地琢磨，游弋沉浸于原文和译文之中，感受着创造的愉悦和乐趣。

　　为了译好本书，我重读了《圣经故事》、相关的英美诗歌和外国文学名著。对于原文中自己感觉似是而非的地方，总是查阅背景资料，字斟句酌，绞尽脑汁，力求把海伦的精彩文字和欢喜悲伤投射到译文之中。有时，对一些简单的词汇，也没有望文生义，而是认真查询。如divided skirt是指"裙裤"而不是"开衩的裙"；而在these vast banks of stone and steel中的"banks"，译为"银行"似乎比"大堤"更妥，所以我将该句译为："那些钢筋和石头砌成的宏伟银行"。总之，翻译于我而言，是工作之外的闲情雅趣，我无惧其孤独枯燥，而怡然自得。就像李宗盛在《致匠心》中所言："一辈子总是还得让一些善意执念推着往前，我们因此能愿意去听从内心的安排，专注做点东西，至少，对得起光阴岁月……"

　　在翻译过程中，我一次又一次地被海伦·凯勒的乐观坚毅所感动；也被她和沙利文老师之间的关爱和友谊所震撼。沙利文老师寓教于乐、循循善诱的教学方法，在今天也很值得我们借鉴和学习。她把大自然当作课堂，让海伦从万事万物中发现美，激发孩子的学习兴趣。在启迪智慧的同时，还用细腻的情感和善良的心性对海伦进行道德教育，让海伦走出了蒙昧和乖戾，成长为一名博学多才、仁爱幸福的杰出女性。

我希望本书的出版能促使更多的人去关注盲聋人的教育权和生存权。1899年，海伦·凯勒曾用盲文试卷答题，并通过了哈佛大学拉德克利夫学院的入学考试。而2014年6月，欣闻中国也有一位盲人首次使用盲文试卷参加了高考。相信海伦·凯勒的事迹定能点亮盲聋人群体的心灵之灯，引领他们走向更加坚强而积极的人生。

感谢挚友马洛红多年来对我的关心和启迪！感谢昆明市外侨办项艳女士对翻译本书所做的贡献！感谢赵庆莲女士的帮助！伴着亲朋好友们的高谊暖语，我愿意在翻译之路上，继续执着而快乐地前行。

查文宏

2014年10月于昆明